28 DAYS TO A BIBLICAL BUSINESS FOUNDATION

A BUSINESS DEVOTIONAL

By R. N. Anderson

28 Days to a Biblical Business Foundation

Copyright © 2020 by R. N. Anderson

Scripture quotations taken from the New American Standard Bible. (NASB),
Copyright © 1960, 1962, 1963, 1968, 1971, 1972, 1973,
1975, 1977, 1995 by The Lockman Foundation
Used by permission. www.Lockman.org

Book and Cover design by R. N. Anderson
ISBN: 978-1-941102-16-9

First Edition : December 2020

INTRODUCTION

A Brief Word

This book is written for the business owner, and for the student who one day might become a business owner or work for a Christ-following organization. In my years of searching for practical knowledge of the Bible that can be applied to everyday business, I have found many deep things and a lot of fluff. Our own hearts and those leading us can often give us false information that sounds logical, but, in fact, is a distortion of God's word. The purpose of this book is to surround you with God's truth in order to help you call out the lies that easily slip their way into business and our beliefs.

1 Peter 5:8-9

> *8 Be of sober spirit, be on the alert. Your adversary, the devil, prowls around like a roaring lion, seeking someone to devour. 9 But resist him, firm in your faith, knowing that the same experiences of suffering are being accomplished by your brethren who are in the world.*

We are to always be watching and be ready to stand firm in our faith. This book is not meant to be a rebuke to any specific person, but will become one to many. On many occasions, I found God's word rebuking me and my disbelief as I wrote it. I use many examples because I want you to be aware of how easily these thoughts can creep into any organization. Many of them may even seem Christ-like, but we must remember that God sees the heart behind our actions. This book is to help you meet with God and discover the truth He has for you as you guide your business.

I love the Bible, and am almost as equally passionate about business. I will discuss both at any given opportunity. I write with more comic relief for myself than for others, but I have included bits of it for those who need the chuckle while digging into what the Word of God has for you. The rest of you serious readers can keep cruising, I won't be offended.[1]

For some of you, my words will come as a reminder to what you have learned, for others, it might come as a full affront to what you've been taught, or the "aha" moment you needed to put your finger on the problems you've been having. I have been told I can be abrasive, but in full honesty, I love conflict! As long as conflict results in productivity, I willingly grapple with it.

My attention span is short, however. I try to stuff as many thoughts as possible into small punches. I drink from the firehose, and proceed to wrestle it out with God. I wish for you the same. If you have a problem with something I've written, I pray that you and God dig into the word together and strengthen your understanding of the truth.

He will lead us if we let Him. He will show us if we seek Him. He will blow our minds when we choose to trust Him. In sickness or health, poverty or wealth, good economics or bad, life and death, He will use all to bring glory to His name alone. He will not share that glory, and we should get out of the way to let Him have it in our lives and in our businesses.

May the Lord be magnified!

---

[1] I will probably not offend you as well! It's a win-win really.

DAY 1

The Biblical Purpose of Business

Before we define why we personally are in business and what our goals should be, it is imperative that we first define what God's ultimate goal is. Why is this so important? Because without a full understanding of God's goal, we cannot even begin to understand our own. Let's check out a few verses that give us hints to God's goal across the scope of the Bible.

Genesis 11:4-9

4 They said, "Come, let us build for ourselves a city, and a tower whose top will reach into heaven, and let us make for ourselves a name, otherwise we will be scattered abroad over the face of the whole earth." 5 The Lord came down to see the city and the tower which the sons of men had built. 6 The Lord said, "Behold, they are one people, and they all have the same language. And this is what they began to do, and now nothing which they purpose to do will be impossible for them. 7 Come, let Us go down and there confuse their language, so that they will not understand one another's speech." 8 So the Lord scattered them abroad from there over the face of the whole earth; and they stopped building the city. 9 Therefore its name was called Babel, because there the Lord confused the language of the whole earth; and from there the Lord scattered them abroad over the face of the whole earth.

Exodus 14:18

18 Then the Egyptians will know that I am the Lord, when I am honored through Pharaoh, through his chariots and his horsemen."

Psalms 50:15

15 Call upon Me in the day of trouble; I shall rescue you, and you will honor Me."

Isaiah 48:9-11

9 "For the sake of My name I delay My wrath, And for My praise I restrain it for you, In order not to cut you off. 10 "Behold, I have refined you, but not as silver; I have tested you in the furnace of affliction. 11 "For My own sake, for My own sake, I will act; For how can My name be profaned? And My glory I will not give to another.

Jeremiah 13:11

11 For as the waistband clings to the waist of a man, so I made the whole household of Israel and the whole household of Judah cling to Me,' declares the Lord, 'that they might be for Me a people, for renown, for praise and for glory; but they did not listen.'

Ephesians 1:10b-12

In Him 11 also we have obtained an inheritance, having been predestined according to His purpose who works all things after the counsel of His will, 12 to the end that we who were the first to hope in Christ would be to the praise of His glory.

1 Corinthians 10:31

31 Whether, then, you eat or drink or whatever you do, do all to the glory of God.

It should be clear by this point throughout the scriptures that we have read (and the many more that I have not mentioned) that God seeks glory for His name alone. Not just from one person either! He seeks glory from all nations. If you need more proof of this, read the Bible and highlight everything He says about His name being worshiped by all nations. His goal is to extend His glory. Does he want us to play a part in glorifying Him? Yes! If He didn't, He wouldn't have sent His son to die for our sins.

So, what does success look like in a Christ follower's life? I asked this question to some ladies recently saying, "What does it mean to have lived a successful life? What does it look like to be able to review your life and say, 'Yes, my life was a success'?"

The answer took them less than 5 minutes to come up with. A successful life is one that has been used to glorify God. Pointing to God in all that we do is something that should be our focus as Christians. So how does this affect business?

We should be in business for the sole purpose of glorifying God.

Every decision in how we conduct ourselves through business should start with the question, **"Is this God glorifying?"** If you have felt God's hand on your life to start a business or hope to run your business by a biblical standard, then this is the first question we should be asking ourselves.

Today is short, because I want you to take time to reflect and write down how God can be glorified in your life. We will be covering quite a few practical business examples of this throughout this book, but it's good to start with what your initial impressions are of God using your life for His glory.

Today:

- Write all the ways, personally and professionally, your life is being used for God's glory. Are there any Bible passages that support your thoughts?
- Read them in context and see if they are still consistent with your first thoughts.
- Take a moment to praise the Lord for choosing you to bring Him glory.
- Thank Him for being worthy of our praise.
- Ask that God would help you to point to Him in every sphere of your life.

DAY 2

Setting Our Expectations

In business, I see people who have read a lot about a particular subject matter and are ready to dive in. They usually have set their expectations high and their budget low. I always have to work through the process helping them reframe what is actually possible with the amount of money they are willing to spend and where they are currently starting from.

Otherwise, their excitement quickly wanes and their satisfaction plummets. We know a good business should never over promise or under deliver, so why do we put up with it in Christianity? Half-baked Christianity promises success just to get you in the door, but never actually prepares you for the truth.

Many times, this sets people up to respond exactly how the disciples did who followed Jesus after the feeding of the 5,000. It was free and it was good! Jesus will meet my every future need because He can just multiply bread whenever He wants! Jesus calls out their insincere expectations.

John 6:26

> *26 Jesus answered them and said, "Truly, truly, I say to you, you seek Me, not because you saw signs, but because you ate of the loaves and were filled.*

At this point, I can imagine hundreds of people following Jesus around. He hits them with some pretty hard teachings about being the bread of life to test their sincerity.

John 6:53-58

> *53 So Jesus said to them, "Truly, truly, I say to you, unless you eat the flesh of the Son of Man and drink His blood, you have no life in yourselves. 54 He who eats My flesh and drinks My blood has eternal life, and I will raise him up on the last day.55 For My flesh is true food, and My blood is true drink. 56 He who eats My flesh and drinks My blood abides in Me, and I in him. 57 As the living Father sent Me, and I live because of the Father, so he who eats Me, he also will live because of Me. 58 This is the bread which came down out of heaven; not as the fathers ate and died; he who eats this bread will live forever."*

A lot of people just got grossed out.[2] I would be too if He hadn't clarified in verse 58 that this bread is not like your fathers ate. If we read further, we find He is referring to spiritual bread. These statements are pretty bold and have a dramatic effect.

John 6:66-69

> *66 As a result of this many of His disciples withdrew and were not walking*

---

[2] I'm just going to say, if there was a guy who made bumper stickers with Jesus slogans, this would be a great opportunity for something like, "Jesus' Eternal Bakery: It's Finger Lickin' Good!" "Mano a Manna" or "Cannibalism is The New Spiritual." Okay, sorry. The bread of life jokes just get me going sometimes!

with Him anymore. 67 So Jesus said to the twelve, "You do not want to go away also, do you?" 68 Simon Peter answered Him, "Lord, to whom shall we go? You have words of eternal life. 69 We have believed and have come to know that You are the Holy One of God."

All the disciples leave, but twelve! Talk about seeing your fans disengage! The ones that did stay caught what He was talking about. His words were the key to having eternal life. They believed and had come to know that He was God. They weren't just sticking around for another free meal.

Jesus didn't care if He lost insincere followers, even if it meant the masses left. He might have been sad, but to teach them would be a waste of time. Our relationship with God will be unstable unless we truly count the cost to follow Him and understand where we are in our current state. We must frame our expectations according to the Bible or our excitement will wane and our satisfaction will plummet.

As exciting as it is to understand how God can shape your business, we must cover some core basics in our understanding first. There are three major things we must know for certain. If we do not establish them now, much of the pages that follow could come as a shock or a disappointment to you.

1. The definition of good
2. What the gospel means
3. What following Jesus looks like

In the book of Mark, a man came to Jesus to get His stamp of approval and found far more about these 3 areas than he bargained for.

Mark 10:17-22

17 As He was setting out on a journey, a man ran up to Him and knelt before Him, and asked Him, "Good Teacher, what shall I do to inherit eternal life?" 18 And Jesus said to him, "Why do you call Me good? No one is good except

*God alone. **19** You know the commandments, 'Do not murder, Do not commit adultery, Do not steal, Do not bear false witness, Do not defraud, Honor your father and mother.'" **20** And he said to Him, "Teacher, I have kept all these things from my youth up." **21** Looking at him, Jesus felt a love for him and said to him, "One thing you lack: go and sell all you possess and give to the poor, and you will have treasure in heaven; and come, follow Me." **22** But at these words he was saddened, and he went away grieving, for he was one who owned much property.*

Only God is good. Even if we have lived the best lives we think possible and run to the feet of Jesus, excited to hear what else we can do to inherit the kingdom of Heaven, He will still tell us, "Only God is good."

If only God is good, we must not be capable of true goodness outside of God. In fact, when we look at who the world claims to consider good, we realize that every good act in the world's eyes is not truly pure goodness, for it always comes with the pleasure of satisfying ourselves in merely seeing the goodness enacted. Altruism is, in fact, self-satisfying. Why? Because we lust in the flesh and are naturally children of wrath.

Ephesians 2:1-3

1 And you were dead in your trespasses and sins, 2 in which you formerly walked according to the course of this world, according to the prince of the power of the air, of the spirit that is now working in the sons of disobedience. 3 Among them we too all formerly lived in the lusts of our flesh, indulging the desires of the flesh and of the mind, and were by nature children of wrath, even as the rest.

Isaiah 64:6

6 For all of us have become like one who is unclean, And all our righteous deeds are like a filthy garment; And all of us wither like a leaf, And our iniquities, like the wind, take us away.

Sin makes us incapable of goodness outside of God. Our goodness is so distorted that it is like a filthy garment to God. My mental picture of this is similar to a cat bringing an owner the tribute of a dead mouse. We consider our efforts good, but the Lord sees the infestation of fleas we have brought Him as outside of His true goodness. We must come to the knowledge of who we are before a Holy God in order to truly appreciate the reconciliation that Jesus brought us.

The Gospel. The gospel is the story of God who took on flesh to live a sinless life. He offered Himself as a sacrifice for our sins to satisfy a Father that demands justice. In His sinless nature, was not bound to death, but defeated the grave to live eternally and to reign with God. Because of this, He now can bring us into a right relationship with the Father when we acknowledge our sin, confess our belief in Him as Lord, and believe He is the risen son of God.

Some of you more "mature" Christians have heard this so many times that you just skimmed the last paragraph. Your head knowledge is not impressing anyone. If you truly get this, how is it impacting your heart? This is everything. Without it, this book is utterly useless. When is the last time you were moved to tears because of the gospel?[3]

The gospel is a rescue mission of love on our behalf, enacted while we were still fighting against God. While we were still in ruthless rebellion against our creator, He chose to save us. The man we read about earlier, who sought Jesus, thought that he was already good. When he finds that he is lacking, he does not want to fully commit in order to inherit the kingdom of heaven. We commonly flirt with the gospel, but refuse to make an all-out commitment in having Jesus as Lord of our lives. Jesus looked at this rich property owner and loved him. If we truly want Jesus to impact our business, we need to surrender everything to the Lord or we will only trick ourselves into thinking we are doing great.

Following Jesus. Following Jesus has come to most people in our nation as a convenient

---

[3] I know exactly who you are because I am right there with you on too many occasions. May we refuse to let our knowledge make us numb to its meaning.

option that seems to fit with their historical background and traditions. To follow Him and accept His love is to have a joyful life in the future. The simple act of completing confirmation classes or even baptism has been your spiritual band aid that will cover all. "I have recognized my sin before God, and He has saved me. Check!" Then, many of us have moved on.

However, if we truly seek to follow the Lord, Jesus describes this journey far different than most quick Easter and Christmas sermons we've attended.

Luke 9:23-26

> *23 And He was saying to them all, "If anyone wishes to come after Me, he must deny himself, and take up his cross daily and follow Me. 24 For whoever wishes to save his life will lose it, but whoever loses his life for My sake, he is the one who will save it. 25 For what is a man profited if he gains the whole world, and loses or forfeits himself? 26 For whoever is ashamed of Me and My words, the Son of Man will be ashamed of him when He comes in His glory, and the glory of the Father and of the holy angels.*

Jackie Hill Perry points out that most of us miss the excruciating nature of crucifixion in this passage.[4] Jesus isn't just saying that following Him will be unpleasant sometimes. He's pointing out that it can be agonizing, daily. If we are to grasp this concept without first understanding the incredible love of God and our crippling sin, some of you would be walking away right now. Make no mistake, however, following Jesus will be hard.

A relationship with God is captivating, incredible, mind blowing, and miraculous, but none of that will be experienced if we fail to follow the Lord. True acknowledgement of our sin and confession of our need for Christ as our savior should lead to life transformation. Dying to ourselves and following Him isn't a one and done moment in time, it is a lifetime of living in goodness because God is the only one that is good.

---

[4] Perry, J. H. (2018). Gay girl, good God: The story of who I was and who God has always been. Nashville, TN: B&H Publishing Group.

This understanding will affect our view of business dramatically. It will transform our businesses and our hearts into something that others will look at one day and be able to see the Lord's work and praise God. If our sole purpose is to glorify God, and the purpose of business is to allow us to do that, then our expectations must be grounded in understanding the fullness of who He is, the weight of our eternal separation and despair, and what the gospel has given us.

Today:

- Take time to praise God for making you free.
- Praise God that He doesn't over promise or underdeliver.
- Confess to God your sin and the times you have thought you could be good without Him.
- Thank the Lord for loving you even while you were still dead in your sin.
- Ask the Lord to help you set your expectations for business into alignment with who He is and what He has done for you.
- Pray that God would firmly root you in His word so that you will not be shaken when your cross is painful.
- Praise God for seeing past your excitement and calling you to prepare for the road ahead.

DAY 3

God's Plan Is Not Designed by You

For many of us who run a business or hope to someday, we are action oriented. We see the future potential and get so excited. The first thing we must do to set about attaining the future is to act. I am no stranger to this urge.

Recently, a nearby town had a mystery hunt to find a hidden winter coin (it's a clear, shiny piece of plastic that looks cool). If you found it, you would win $500. Each day, a new clue was released regarding its location. My husband and my father-in-law wanted to research the clues by Googling different names that the clues provided. I, on the other hand, decided we must act now! I wanted to get in the car and go looking.

I was ready to head out to the cemetery across town because it hinted to a soldier's memorial. I was frustrated that no one was moving. They were content to sit there and do nothing, but research! After another 5 minutes of my passive aggressive huffs, they discovered that the clue actually pointed to the high school's Veterans Memorial and not the cemetery.

I had had it! I left to go to the Veterans Memorial. Even as I was there, they found the other clues were pointing onward. My husband said, "You would have been at the Soldier's Memorial across town if you wouldn't have waited 5 minutes longer."

Frustrated,[5] I called my father-in-law. He was at home, still doing research, while I drove around. Within another 15 minutes, the clues brought me to my final destination. I was once again, back. DIRECTLY ACROSS THE STREET from my in-law's house. This was approximately 30 minutes after my initial frustration.[6]

Sometimes in business, we find ourselves beside the burden we've been hauling up the stairs one step at a time, exhausted and frustrated. In my head, I can imagine God walking by and saying something similar to, "I can see you've worked really hard on this, but why didn't you use the elevator I installed?" Doing things in business God's way usually means a lot more waiting than we mentally prepare ourselves for.

Here's the truth: When God wants something to happen, He makes it happen.

Throughout the Psalms we see many times the writer is in despair. There are continual outcries to God throughout the writings. The response to these, however, is very interesting. There is never a moment where the writer says, "I was struggling, so I went out, and solved the problem."

Instead, we find a completely different response. Let's check some of these out:

---

[5] Mostly because I knew he was right!

[6] We never found the medallion. Someone had already beaten us to it. All we got was an opportunity to improve our marriage and communication habits!

Psalms 27: 12-14

12 Do not deliver me over to the desire of my adversaries, For false witnesses have risen against me, And such as breathe out violence. 13 I would have despaired unless I had believed that I would see the goodness of the Lord In the land of the living. 14 Wait for the Lord; Be strong and let your heart take courage; Yes, wait for the Lord.

Psalms 37:7-8, 34

7 Rest in the Lord and wait patiently for Him; Do not fret because of him who prospers in his way, Because of the man who carries out wicked schemes. 8 Cease from anger and forsake wrath; Do not fret; it leads only to evildoing...34 Wait for the Lord and keep His way, And He will exalt you to inherit the land; When the wicked are cut off, you will see it.

Psalms 59:1, 9, 16-17

1 Deliver me from my enemies, O my God; Set me securely on high away from those who rise up against me...9 Because of his strength I will watch for You, For God is my stronghold...16 But as for me, I shall sing of Your strength; Yes, I shall joyfully sing of Your lovingkindness in the morning, For You have been my stronghold And a refuge in the day of my distress. 17 O my strength, I will sing praises to You; For God is my stronghold, the God who shows me loving kindness.

Psalms 62:1-2

1 My soul waits in silence for God only; From Him is my salvation. 2 He only is my rock and my salvation, My stronghold; I shall not be greatly shaken.

Time and time again, we see a pattern in the Psalms, "When there is struggle, I wait on the Lord." I want you to go back and read these passages again. This time, I would like you to identify what else we are supposed to do while waiting. Here are some of the ones I picked up on:

- Wait AND
- Let your heart take courage.
- Fret not.
- Keep His way.
- Sing of His strength.
- Sing praises to Him.
- Do not be shaken.

Waiting doesn't mean we sit around and do nothing. No, but it does mean that planning and prayerfully preparing our steps is a part of ensuring God is at the center of each decision. As you start to establish standards, create processes, or implement new ideas, you must ensure that it's the right time to take on each project. At times, there will be things on your priority list that might not be business, but being open to them allows you to be glorifying to God in other areas of your life. These should be considered a blessing to be embraced, not a stressor.

Remember yesterday's question? Is this God glorifying? If the answer is yes, the next question is: **Have I done all I can do to prepare the way for God's plan?**

When given the opportunity to let God's plan play out, we see the path was far more peaceful than our own.

Today:
- Thank God that His plan is always better.
- Praise Him for being in control of everything.
- Take time to pray about the plan that you think He has called you to. Write it down, and save it. (This step is important because as you seek God's guidance, you will look back on this later and realize how so many of your initial perspectives have been shifted or refined by God!)
- Ask God to show you what you can do to help you prepare for where He is calling you.
- Ask that God would help you do them in His timing and with His efficiency.

DAY 4

God's Provision

When I first set up my business, it wasn't something I really ever saw myself doing. I was nervous and uncertain, but God was very clear about the path I needed to take. My husband and I sat down and worked out our finances. We decided that even if I didn't make any money for the first six months, we would be fine. So, I set about on the adventure of government paperwork, legal contracts, and becoming an "official business."

Three months into the adventure of my business, my husband's car came to a place where we had put more money into fixing it than it was worth. The dealer's service department manager pulled me aside and made it clear that we should start looking for a new car. I was stretched! Here we had to start discussing new cars and while I'm quick to act, I know that I'm also quick to buy something that "appears nice" without doing all the background work. I'd hold up my phone to show a Craigslist ad for a car that looked nice. He would patiently look at it, and say something along the lines of, "No, that year is known for transmission issues."

Firstly, I knew I was out of my element. Secondly, I knew this would drain almost everything from our finances. The only thing I could do was pray. I prayed hard that God would guide my husband to find a car that was within budget and going to last a long time.

One day, he called me and said, "Okay, I know we've been looking at a few options, but I really think this one is the answer."

It was a four-hour drive from our house, and I was so nervous. *What if it's junk and we break down on the way back?!* The entire trip there and back I was praying for that car. We made it home, and it has worked wonderfully ever since! The real miracle for me, however, was what followed. Even with our finances low, we felt moved to intensively pay off student debt. We became Dave Ramsey readers and started buckling down.

I told God, "Look, we want to do this, but you need to provide."

In the same time frame, we decided to stop putting off the call to get into foster care! We suddenly had two children added to our meal ticket, and we were going to start paying down debt aggressively. Since that day, God has miraculously provided!

Random people started giving us things they no longer needed. We got bunk beds for the kids, 3 dressers, two mattresses, and a load of unwanted items from someone that was moving and needed to get rid of them (some of which we were able to sell or gift to others in need). To top that all off, we have been able to pay off an additional $13,000 in student debt in a 4-month period. To date, I have no idea how we did this. The numbers still don't make sense.

Do you know what is the crazy thing about all of this? We're now 7 months into my business, still financially in the black, and I haven't taken any money out of the business to pay myself yet. Let me tell you, I have tried hard to contribute to my family's finances! I tried taking on a second job and was continually finding new excuses to stop running my business and make money elsewhere. I would get upset along the way because I felt like dead weight, but God kept closing all the doors to help me "contribute."

God spoke to my heart and said, "You know that if you got a second job and it worked out, you would give up your business, right?" *Agh! This was so true! This was my secret excuse plan I didn't even want to admit to myself!*

A few weeks later, He followed it up with, "You know that if I let you contribute financially, you would think you did this all on your own." *Is this consistent with what I know of God? Yes! All of this is for His glory, and not mine! This whole time I have been stressing about my stair by stair effort, when God's been riding the elevator up and down ten times over!*

I was reminded that God seeks to provide for us in His way and in His timing by a passage in Matthew.

Matthew 7:7-10

> 7 *"Ask, and it will be given to you; seek, and you will find; knock, and it will be opened to you. 8 For everyone who asks receives, and he who seeks finds, and to him who knocks it will be opened. 9 Or what man is there among you who, when his son asks for a loaf, will give him a stone? 10 Or if he asks for a fish, he will not give him a snake, will he?*

So, here's the distinction that I want to make with this passage. Jesus keeps talking afterwards. Verses 12-14 follow:

Matthew 7:12-14

> 12 *"In everything, therefore, treat people the same way you want them to treat you, for this is the Law and the Prophets. 13 "Enter through the narrow gate; for the gate is wide and the way is broad that leads to destruction, and there are many who enter through it. 14 For the gate is small and the way is narrow that leads to life, and there are few who find it.*

The path to following Christ versus following the world is harder than we make it out to be. We don't just ask what we want from God and expect everything to be easy while He grants it. I had to come to terms with the fact that in my business, I was trying to choose what I thought was the easiest way to "fulfilling God's calling in my life." The path of least resistance sure looks a lot like the wide gate! See, just because Jesus says that we should ask doesn't mean that we will find or receive what we thought we would. The reality is, we're going to get what God knows we need to experience the fullness of His goodness.

Sometimes what we need is physical pain in order to be refined. Sometimes what we need is limited finances to be able to rely on His faithfulness. God is not a genie in a bottle. He did not come to give you your heart's desire so people can see how great you are. He is after His own glory. He will give us whatever we need to bring Him glory for a season or a lifetime if it is necessary to magnify His name.

We have to be headed down the path with the narrow gate in order to see the blessings He wants to provide us with. Let's identify that the way is hard that leads to life. If it wasn't, we'd see a whole lot more people living out the call to follow Christ. The point is, God wants us to experience His goodness.

Ecclesiastes 6:3-6

> *3 If a man fathers a hundred children and lives many years, however many they be, but his soul is not satisfied with good things and he does not even have a proper burial, then I say, "Better the miscarriage than he, 4 for it comes in futility and goes into obscurity; and its name is covered in obscurity. 5 It never sees the sun and it never knows anything; it is better off than he. 6 Even if the other man lives a thousand years twice and does not enjoy good things—do not all go to one place?"*

We know already, only God is good. If we go our entire life with having everything or having nothing and never truly experience the goodness of God, our life was wasted.

To truly experience God's goodness leads to telling other people about it. You won't be able to help it. Your enjoyment will not be complete until you feel you have shared it with someone else in the world. In fact, we do this with everything in our lives. We leave reviews, post pictures, share recipes, make our friends watch YouTube videos we enjoyed, and unbearably stifle our laugher in quiet places (only to use hand gestures and whispers to share our amusement with the person next to us). If we experience the goodness of God, it will overflow into a natural retelling of what God has done. This is praise. We cannot help it. This in turn, gives God the glory due His name.

The path of least resistance naturally flows to the wide gate because it's short sighted and easy. This does not lead us to our ultimate enjoyment. There is nothing good outside of God. God wants us to have ultimate enjoyment in Him. His provision allows us to experience enjoyment. If we attribute His provision to someone or something else, He is not receiving His glory. Following Christ is sometimes scary, but when we step out, He loves showing us new ways to praise Him and tell others about His goodness.

Don't settle for less than His goodness. Taking the path that seems less stressful usually happens when we aren't trusting God to come through or because we have not spent enough time discerning the Lord's direction in prayer. This robs us of enjoyment and robs God of praise. I challenge you to dig into the word of God for yourself. Look at what scripture has to say, not other people's opinions of scripture.

Today:
- Thank God for loving us enough to demand our enjoyment of true goodness. Praise God for being who He is.
- Ask God to reveal to you the areas of least resistance that you have been trying to take your business.
- Pray that God would show you how to seek only His goodness.
- Ask God to direct your focus to the narrow gate and strip down the thoughts you have over complicated in trying to get there.
- Repent to God for forgetting what His words says about His love and provision for us.
- Ask God to show you how to remind yourself of His provision when you have doubts.
- Pray that God would give you opportunities to trust in His provision and to experience His goodness.

DAY 5

Vulnerability

Setting up your business, according to God, is a personal and collective journey. You see, when you fall more and more in love with God, it changes the way you respond to those around you. Your quest to discover more of who God is will result in many other abilities that you never knew God could develop your life. Many times, however, in our sheer will to try to do things on our own, we fail to seek out others who can help us refine those abilities faster.

The Bible is very clear on two points that are common pitfalls for business owners: Pride and Seeking Wisdom. These two go hand in hand for many people. If you have pride, it's unlikely you will be vulnerable enough to seek wisdom strategically.

There are many people that attempt to seek guidance through gaining knowledge and understanding. They do research, find out answers, and come to a good decision. This can turn into the minutes saved and hours wasted approach. Afterwards, this can even continue to fuel their pride. They feel self-sufficient. *Why do I need anyone else when I can find the answer myself?*

Proverbs 4:7

> *7 "The beginning of wisdom is: Acquire wisdom; And with all your acquiring, get understanding.*

Proverbs 8:12-13

> *12 "I, wisdom, dwell with prudence, And I find knowledge and discretion. 13 "The fear of the Lord is to hate evil; Pride and arrogance and the evil way And the perverted mouth, I hate.*

Proverbs 11:2

> *2 When pride comes, then comes dishonor, But with the humble is wisdom.*

Isaiah 2:12

> *12 For the Lord of hosts will have a day of reckoning Against everyone who is proud and lofty And against everyone who is lifted up, That he may be abased.*

James 4:6-10

> *6 But He gives a greater grace. Therefore it says, "God is opposed to the proud, but gives grace to the humble." 7 Submit therefore to God. Resist the devil and he will flee from you. 8 Draw near to God and He will draw near to you. Cleanse your hands, you sinners; and purify your hearts, you double-minded. 9 Be miserable and mourn and weep; let your laughter be turned into mourning and your joy to gloom. 10 Humble yourselves in the presence of the Lord, and He will exalt you.*

Firstly, we find that seeking wisdom is a big deal to God. Secondly, wisdom is found in humility. Thirdly, God happens to hate pride. He actually bold face opposes and has a special day ("The Day of Reckoning") for all that are too proud to receive wisdom. From what we've read so far, I am feeling a bit more nervous than I did before about my own heart. These are pretty harsh words for those that think they can do it all.

The beauty of God's plan for our lives is that we are not doing it alone. In the very first chapters of the Bible (Gen. 2:18), God said, "It is not good that man should be alone." Do you think this would differ as we stepped into business? God wants us to be in communication with others about our needs so that we can receive wisdom.

Proverbs 11:14

14 Where there is no guidance the people fall, But in abundance of counselors there is victory.

Proverbs 15:22

22 Without consultation, plans are frustrated, But with many counselors they succeed.

Proverbs 24:6

6 For by wise guidance you will wage war, And in abundance of counselors there is victory.

Seeking guidance is something that can be more difficult than we anticipate because we mentally complicate it. We think things like:

- Well, they don't know anything about business.
- I don't want to be a burden.
- What if they tell my competition?
- They are really busy. Now's not the right time.
- I need to be a wise steward of my finances, and advice can get costly.
- I don't want them to think I'm taking advantage of them.
- I don't want to tell people about my financial situation.
- Other people's problems are bigger than this.

- I'm not sure how to word it, so it will be too confusing for others to understand.
- If I tell someone I'm struggling, I might lose credibility with my customers or colleagues.

Ask yourself: **Does God care about these things more than your obedience?**
Most of those excuses revolve around you saving face or sending yourself on a guilt trip. Pride and false modesty are beating you at every chance of efficiency within your business.

Also, did I mention that those who are believers in Christ have the ability to pray for your business when they hear about it? Can you put a dollar value on prayer? If you can, then you might need to get a good lesson from Simon the Sorcerer in Acts 8. Prayer is the most powerful thing we can do for our business. It's the most powerful thing others can do for our business.

Today:

- Ask God to reveal who you should be seeking guidance from in your business and personal life.
- Repent from any false justification that has kept you from humbling yourself before God and seeking council.
- Thank God that He has not designed us to go through life without community and encouragement.
- Make a list of all the people you need to be praying for, and set calendar dates for yourself to follow up with them about what God has been doing. You need the accountability to pray, and they need the prayers.
- Ask God to continue to show you the prayer requests other people have and go before God in intercession for them.
- Pray that God would work in your heart to be vulnerable with others about what's going on in your life and business.
- Praise God that He is the defender of the weak and will protect us in our vulnerability.

DAY 6

The Concept of Control

When I need to get things done, the first thing I do is write down a list. It probably has something to do with the fact that my StrengthsFinder tells me I am a high achiever. I must check things off in order to feel I have accomplished something. I need to physically watch myself check off a task to feel endorphins. It's how God made me. When I don't get anything done on my list, by the end of the day I'm ready to have a meltdown. It's defeating and overwhelming.

Sometimes part of the reason I didn't get anything done is because there were so many other unexpected things that happened in my day. I had to make a quick run to the pharmacy, the dog threw up everywhere, my washer started overflowing into the basement, Google Search Console told me that it doesn't like my website, a potential client call turned into a 2-hour heart to heart, the list keeps going.

Our day can get out of control really quickly. Now, there's a lot of great people out there that will end this statement by saying, "If you let it. The key is to take control of your life!"

Don't worry, we're not going there, because if you really could control your life, then you wouldn't really need God, would you?

When life gets frustrating and out of control, we must remember that the Lord is sovereign. The concept of sovereign is actually very hard for me to grasp. I have struggled with it many times because in my experiences, a lot of really well-intentioned people use it when they are trying to comfort those in bereavement. This makes me want to push whatever sovereignty is out of my way. I think, "If God is that, then He must be unkind!"

When we actually look at the definition of what sovereign is, however, it means something way more understandable than I have made it out to be. The Merriam Webster definition of sovereign is:

a: one possessing or held to possess supreme political power or sovereignty
b: one that exercises supreme authority within a limited sphere
c: an acknowledged leader[7]

By definition then, one who is sovereign has supreme control or authority. How should this affect our view of daily life and who God says He is? Let's check out the word of God for further understanding of how God's supreme power plays out on a regular basis.

Proverbs 16:3-4

3 Commit your works to the Lord And your plans will be established. 4 The Lord has made everything for its own purpose, Even the wicked for the day of evil.

Proverbs 19:21

21 Many plans are in a man's heart, But the counsel of the Lord will stand.

---

[7] Sovereign. (2019) Retrieved March 18, 2019, from https://www.merriam-webster.com/dictionary/sovereign

In what we are reading in Proverbs, we find that God clearly has plans established and a purpose in what He is doing. Verse 3 of chapter 16 does point out that we do play a part in dedicating our work to the Lord. This is an important point because I believe that God doesn't call us to sit by and watch everything play out. In whatever we do, including business, He can use us for His glory, if we let Him.

In Proverbs 19, we learn that even though we have these plans that we're bringing before the Lord, He is still here to bring about His ultimate purpose and not ours. Does that mean there is no point in setting growth goals as a business or pushing to find new opportunities in the marketplace because God's plan will ultimately work out anyways? Absolutely not.

Colossians 3:23-25

23 Whatever you do, do your work heartily, as for the Lord rather than for men, 24 knowing that from the Lord you will receive the reward of the inheritance. It is the Lord Christ whom you serve. 25 For he who does wrong will receive the consequences of the wrong which he has done, and that without partiality.

Working hard is a part of worship to God through serving Christ. There are many business books out there that will tell you, "What you put in is what you will get out of your business." I will take a different perspective to this and say, the way you work, and who you are working for will determine what you get out of your business. My hope is that you will understand your inheritance is not about earthly finances here. Paul is talking about our eternal inheritance of a life in Christ. This is hidden with Christ, where we one day will appear with Christ in glory (Colossians 3:1-4).

We must remember that God is in control of everything. He is sovereign over our plans, and as we work hard in our business, His plan is ultimately going to come about for His glory. The way we act and run our business can be an act of worship to God.

Today:

- What is in your life currently that you think is getting in the way of your plans? Pray that God would reveal these areas to you.

- Do you think that the way you are handling these unexpected "blocks" is honoring to God? Pray that God would remind you of who is in control when these instances arise.

- Do you think that these unexpected instances were a surprise to God? Pray God would work in your heart to recognize His divine sovereignty regularly.

- How do you think God can use these opportunities to display His glory? Pray that God can use you in His plan to glorify Himself.

- How do you think your desire for control inhibits your ability to trust God's plan? Pray that God would help you relinquish control into His hands as you work heartily to serve Christ.

DAY 7

Knowing What to Do

There was a time in my life where I was living far away from everyone I knew and loved. I was working 80-hour weeks, and dealing with the worst business culture I had ever seen. After a few trips home on my odd days off to see family, I was questioned by someone, who had never had a meeting with me before, about what I was doing in my spare time that could put a strain on me and my performance at work.

I was told I wasn't professional in my communication, with only one example given of these occurrences and no clear directives for how to improve. There were clear questions being asked to dig into my personal life to know why I was traveling in my time off. I was told I had 30 days to improve or I would be shown the door.

I left that meeting thinking, "Improve what?" I was given no guidance in my job by those around me; and my external support system had little to no experience in the business world to offer me advice. Every time I would communicate an issue I was seeking help with at work, it became another reason why they should fire me.

I felt like a fish out of water every day. I went home every day pleading with God to tell me what to do. I wept, I lost almost all my body fat from not having time to eat, and felt utterly in despair. I tried to call people and ask them what I should do, but no one had an answer.

"Yeah, that's tough. I'll pray for you," was the response I got from friends and family.

What does God actually want me to do? This is a question we all have on a regular basis. I can tell you that in the last year, I've probably asked this question at least once a day. The questions that rack our brain can include:

- Am I not listening?
- Is He silent?
- What am I supposed to be learning?
- How should I be seeking Him?
- Is this me thinking this or is this from God?
- Am I crazy?

God has many ways of speaking to people and confirming or denying our intuition. For each person it can be different. In that time of my life, I distinctly remember experiencing complete silence. While in this strange silence, I listened to a sermon that gave the testimony of a man who had lost his entire business in a fire, one child to sickness, and the rest of his children in a vacation accident. In his grief, he traveled to where his children had perished and started to praise the Lord. Even in his grief, he knew that he had freedom from eternal death. He knew without God, he was helpless. Jesus chose to die for him, and for that, he praised the Lord. His choice to praise the Lord in the midst of sadness and uncertainty made me realize this is what God wants from us! Even when we don't know what to do, we need to praise the Lord.

Psalms 92:1-5

1 It is good to give thanks to the Lord And to sing praises to Your name, O Most High; 2 To declare Your lovingkindness in the morning And Your

faithfulness by night, 3 With the ten-stringed lute and with the harp, With
resounding music upon the lyre. 4 For You, O Lord, have made me glad by
what You have done, I will sing for joy at the works of Your hands. 5 How
great are Your works, O Lord! Your thoughts are very deep.

Regardless of the intuition and gut feelings that we may get or never receive, the word of
God is always true and living. It tells us what we should be doing. Verse 2 says we are to
declare His love in the morning and His faithfulness by night.

Praising the Lord and lifting your prayers to Him in the midst of uncertainty is a scary
subject for many people. What if God never tells us what to do and we just have to make our
own choice? Hello! The word of God tells us what to do all the time! It might not be the
exact answer we wanted to hear, but it will guide us to what God wants us to focus on.

Philippians 4:4-7

4 Rejoice in the Lord always; again I will say, rejoice! 5 Let your gentle spirit
be known to all men. The Lord is near. 6 Be anxious for nothing, but in
everything by prayer and supplication with thanksgiving let your requests be
made known to God. 7 And the peace of God, which surpasses all
comprehension, will guard your hearts and your minds in Christ Jesus.

We are to pray with thanksgiving. Supplication is the action of humbly or continually
asking/begging. He will also give us peace to guard our hearts when we make our requests
known to Him.

An additional note I would like to make about being guided by God: If your gut instinct or
intuition is contradictory to the word of God, it is not from God. There's no need to pray any
further. God will not call you to make a decision that is contradictory to His word. Ever. You
should immediately dismiss that option as a "no" from God. Dwelling on it further gives you
the opportunity to twist the truth and justify your actions. This is wrong. You will feel guilt

and shame when you try to justify it to other Christ followers,[8] and it will end in regret, consequences, or lost opportunities for God to bless and sanctify your life in other areas.

2 Timothy 3:14-17

> *14 You, however, continue in the things you have learned and become convinced of, knowing from whom you have learned them, 15 and that from childhood you have known the sacred writings which are able to give you the wisdom that leads to salvation through faith which is in Christ Jesus. 16 All Scripture is inspired by God and profitable for teaching, for reproof, for correction, for training in righteousness; 17 so that the man of God may be adequate, equipped for every good work.*

God's word is able to teach us, correct us, and train us to be equipped for every good work. God can also use other ways to confirm His guidance for our lives. We spoke about one earlier when we discussed vulnerability. God can confirm His will through the confirmation of other trusted advisors in our lives. He can use dreams, visions, the peace that surpasses understanding (Phil. 4:7), repetition of scripture, wisdom & discernment, and even prophetic word. When you're trying to seek God's will, understanding your motives can be helpful to working through the decision. We must understand that sometimes God doesn't care about the final decision as much as He cares about how we conduct ourselves through it.

Sometimes there will be things that seem like a good thing to do, but aren't actually a part of God's plan for us. This is okay. One time, we were asked to consider the adoption of a child through foster care. Now, we know the book of James says "true religion is this, to look after orphans and widows." So, we prayerfully considered it. We asked others to pray for us. The weird thing about it was that I never got that excited feeling of welcoming this new person

---

[8] Here's a good hint that you're justifying your actions: You are telling people about an amazing opportunity, while hiding the potential and evident downfalls. Hiding a portion of the truth or the risk is a common sign of justification.

into our home. I did care for the child's wellbeing, but something didn't feel like we were actually ready.

I told God, "If no one else can do this, I will. If there is no home, we will be the home."

Finally, God showed us that there were many other families out there excitedly awaiting a child of this age. To agree to an adoption out of obligation, when I knew others were joyfully hoping for this opportunity, was not God's plan for this child. Praise God that He provides a way for what is best! God doesn't ask us to do stuff we have no joy in doing all the time. Will it happen? Sometimes, but God works for the good of those who love Him. He will give us a passion for doing what He has called us to when we ask Him.

As you consider God's will for your life or business, ask yourself the following questions:
- Has God already spoken about something specific that I am supposed to be focusing on?
- Am I doing this to ignore God's other clear commands to me in my life?
- Is this decision in contradiction to or consistent with what the word of God says? (Write down the verses and read them in context of the passages to help you answer this one more clearly.)
- Has God already told me to wait?
- Are my trusted advisors supporting this decision?
- Have I even taken the time to reach out to trusted advisors yet?
- Does what I know to be true contradict the reasoning for this decision?
- Am I making this decision too quickly? Have I spent enough time in prayer and praise over this decision?
- Do I feel peace about this or is it just a sense of relief because I want to be done?
- Does it make wise financial sense for me to do this right now?
- Am I in control of my emotions right now or am I deciding this out of fear, anger, love, excitement, etc.?
- Is this decision fulfilling a clear command of God?
- Is this decision going to align me or bind me to a commitment with those who could alter my decision-making process in the future to be less godly?

- Am I tentative to make this decision because there are clear reservations to why this decision is unwise or is it because my personality is generally more cautious?
- Is my spouse/family in support of this decision?
- Will this decision have negative effects on my family's commitment to following Christ?

Today:

- Look back on the previous questions and pick three to pray through. Ask God to bring clarity to your heart.
- Lay your requests before God and praise Him. Sometimes we are ready to act before fully hearing His message.
- Pray that God would help you to understand His timing.
- Praise Him while you are waiting on His guidance. God might be still speaking.
- Thank God that He will continue to sanctify us and prepare us for what is next as we continually seek Him.

DAY 8

The Clear Command of God

I cannot count the amount of times in business I have heard the words, "I feel like God is saying." The word "feel" is common for our culture. It is how we describe our instincts, intuition, and emotion. Within business, there are many people renowned for their ability to see the winds of change and react. We also marvel at the people who are able to do this with God's leading!

Many times, we act because we feel. But what about addressing the clear commands God has already laid out in the Bible? Some of them are pretty obvious and most of society agrees with them: don't kill, don't lie, don't steal.

The commands Jesus gave us in the New Testament take a bit more work, however. Love your neighbor as yourself, turn the other cheek, and forgive others. These are all personal issues to work on, and quite honestly, we just don't "feel" like doing them sometimes. The clear command of God does not have to be backed by a warm and fuzzy feeling to be true and still a command. Many times, the feelings that accompany commands are actually negative because it is the hard thing to do!

We need to address how your business plays a part in supporting the great commission. The great commission is a clear command that Jesus gave the church. It also was the last thing He said to His disciples before being taken into heaven. From those two facts alone, I think we all can surmise, it was a pretty big deal for Jesus.

I'm just imagining what my last words to my family would be if I left for a big cross-country trip. I'd probably say something pretty trivial that came to my mind, "Don't forget to feed the dog!" or "There's extra pizzas in the freezer in case you need them."

If we know one thing about Jesus, it's that He is always intentional. ALWAYS. I think if I knew this was the last time I were to see my family on earth, I would probably be a bit more intentional too. If I could equate this to a pop culture human equivalent, it'd be like Nicolas Cage phoning his daughter in the remake of the Left Behind movie.[9] No matter what happens to the plane he's flying, with little to no fuel left, she needs to know he loves her.

In three of the four gospels, Jesus gives a pretty clear picture of what the disciples are supposed to do after he leaves them.

Mark 16:15

15 And He said to them, "Go into all the world and preach the gospel to all creation.

Matthew 28:19-20

19 Go therefore and make disciples of all the nations, baptizing them in the name of the Father and the Son and the Holy Spirit, 20 teaching them to

---

[9] My husband will tell you that I think Nicolas Cage only has one facial expression, so it's still hard for me to trust his display of sincerity in any movie. This is a highly debated subject in our house.

observe all that I commanded you; and lo, I am with you always, even to the end of the age."

Luke 24:45-47

45 Then He opened their minds to understand the Scriptures, 46 and He said to them, "Thus it is written, that the Christ would suffer and rise again from the dead the third day, 47 and that repentance for forgiveness of sins would be proclaimed in His name to all the nations, beginning from Jerusalem.

Here's where the majority of the American church has missed the great commission: **all the world, the whole creation, all nations**.

Our concept of missions is equivalent to our concept of ministry. We tell ourselves that the moment we step out of our church building, we have now donned the missionary name tag. Missions and ministry are two different things. We must separate them with the concept of "access." Everyone "needs" Jesus. Not everyone has "access" to Jesus. The gospel is good news to all people, but we haven't done a very good job of proclaiming it to all people.

Before you wave the heresy flag, I do understand there are many places in the world that people receive dreams and visions of Jesus. In reviewing the occurrence of Cornelius having this happen to him in the Bible (and in the many other modern-day instances of people having visions and dreams), visions and dreams usually correlate to a specific instance that pushes one to seek additional information about Christ elsewhere (from specific people such as the apostle Peter, people who claim to be Christians, the Bible itself, the internet, etc.) I believe this comes out of the book of Romans as well.

Romans 10:11-17

11 For the Scripture says, "Whoever believes in Him will not be disappointed." 12 For there is no distinction between Jew and Greek; for the same Lord is Lord of all, abounding in riches for all who call on Him; 13 for "Whoever will call on the name of the Lord will be saved." 14 How then will they call on Him in whom they have not believed? How will they believe in

Him whom they have not heard? And how will they hear without a preacher?
15 How will they preach unless they are sent? Just as it is written, "How
beautiful are the feet of those who bring good news of good things!" 16
However, they did not all heed the good news; for Isaiah says, "Lord, who
has believed our report?" 17 So faith comes from hearing, and hearing by the
word of Christ.

In the past, anyone who has claimed to have a full revelation directly from God, about all the answers to life, has started a new religion, denounced the Bible as the word of God, and replaced it with something else.[10] God can reveal Himself to people, but He uses us to do the discipling part. This idea of spreading the gospel to the entire world isn't new to God's plan. God wants the whole earth to be filled with His glory.

Exodus 9:16

16 But, indeed, for this reason I have allowed you to remain, in order to show
you My power and in order to proclaim My name through all the earth.

Psalm 46:10

10 "Cease striving and know that I am God; I will be exalted among the
nations, I will be exalted in the earth."

The clear command is, "go out into all the earth." From what Jesus said, the purpose is to spread the gospel, and from these verses we know the goal is to glorify God's name throughout all nations.

So, what actually ended up happening to the church in Jerusalem after Jesus left them? We have the Day of Pentecost where many believe because of Peter's testimony. There is

---

[10] Muhammad and Joseph Smith are two noteworthy examples of this.

organizational structure being built to support the local church, but then they all start getting comfortable in Jerusalem. None of them want to leave. Just like we see in Genesis, the Lord forces them to spread out because they're not doing it on their own!

Acts 11:19-26

> *19 So then those who were scattered because of the persecution that occurred in connection with Stephen made their way to Phoenicia and Cyprus and Antioch, speaking the word to no one except to Jews alone. 20 But there were some of them, men of Cyprus and Cyrene, who came to Antioch and began speaking to the Greeks also, preaching the Lord Jesus. 21 And the hand of the Lord was with them, and a large number who believed turned to the Lord. 22 The news about them reached the ears of the church at Jerusalem, and they sent Barnabas off to Antioch. 23 Then when he arrived and witnessed the grace of God, he rejoiced and began to encourage them all with resolute heart to remain true to the Lord; 24 for he was a good man, and full of the Holy Spirit and of faith. And considerable numbers were brought to the Lord. 25 And he left for Tarsus to look for Saul; 26 and when he had found him, he brought him to Antioch. And for an entire year they met with the church and taught considerable numbers; and the disciples were first called Christians in Antioch.*

How your business participates in spreading the gospel is between you and God, but the command is clear that participation is a requirement. Some business owners have done this by offering their services at a discount to those going into ministry. Others do this through visiting missionaries on their vacation, hiring "the least of these," giving of their profits to missions, and training up leaders that can go, using the business skills they have learned.

My husband and I have been working on praying for our missionary workers at 6:30 every morning together. This is a major commitment for a night owl like me, but I have gone from falling asleep regularly over the first month to being able to be cognitive for the entire prayer time (3 months later)!

For a better understanding of what roles there are within "going into all the world," let's define the 5 options.

1. **Praying:** pray for those to go, who are currently serving, and for the nations that still have yet to receive the good news.
2. **Mobilizing:** educating others about God's heart for the nations
3. **Sending:** financially supporting, helping prepare missionaries for their launch, being a part of a home support team for a missionary while they are away.
4. **Going:** reaching the lost who do not have access to the gospel
5. **Welcoming:** inviting those from other nations to be a part of your community who have moved here from abroad

The Joshua Project reports that 41.6% of the world's people groups are considered unreached by the gospel[11], meaning that less than 3% of their entire population knows Christ. Some have no written language, let alone **access** to portions of the Bible or a body of believers.

The majority of the world's unreached people groups reside in what is known as the 10/40 window. The Joshua Project[12] defines this area by saying, "The 10/40 Window is the rectangular area of North Africa, the Middle East and Asia approximately between 10 degrees north and 40 degrees north latitude." This region of the world also has the highest number of countries where proclaiming the gospel is illegal. Missions trips are not welcome, and in fact, are violently rewarded.

The Joshua Project notes that giving to foreign missions for work among unreached people

---

[11] Home. (2019). Joshua Project. Retrieved March 19, 2019, from https://joshuaproject.net/

[12] What is the 10/40 Window?. (2019). Joshua Project. Retrieved March 19, 2019, Retrieved from https://joshuaproject.net/resources/articles/10_40_window

groups is at 1% of the total foreign missions giving.[13] The majority of the United States' missions funding is going to regions of the world that have already been reached by the gospel! They already have access!

Why do I bring up giving? We usually show what we support with our dollars, time, and talents. Why are we, as a Christian community, not reaching the lost who have no access to the map? The reality is, the majority of the world's unreached are located in places we would not feel comfortable sending our local teens for a week-long hiatus. Nor would they actually be effective if we did send them! Have we become so enthralled with the feeling of "doing good" that we have missed what so many have died trying to proclaim?

The command is clear to go to all the earth, the purpose is to proclaim the gospel, the goal is to bring God glory across the earth that every nation and tongue will praise the Lord. I beg you not to miss it and not to base this on a "feeling."

Today:
- Ask God how He is calling you to be a part of His goal to reach the nations.
- Ask God to reveal how He can use your business and local church body to obey Jesus' command.
- Pray that God would not allow your heart to remain stagnant in believing that "need" is equivalent to "access."
- Praise God that He has revealed to us clear commands in the Bible to align our lives around.
- Thank Him for the revelation of His word that we can stand firm in its truth instead of relying on our feelings.

---

[13] Mission Trends and Facts. (2019). Joshua Project. Retrieved March 19, 2019, Retrieved from https://joshuaproject.net/assets/media/handouts/mission-trends-facts.pdf

DAY 9

The Woes of the Business Martyr

Working with passion for your business is hopefully something you are able to do. You do it because it is your life blood. Your commitment to its success is vital to keeping it profitable. Your desire to see success for yourself and others pushes you to give more and more of your time. This can become a dangerous place if you do not tread carefully, however.

Two business partners I once met had an intense dedication to their business, but it came at a price. One working late into the night was shocked when the other didn't show the same dedication to the business in off-hours. Business was their life. Every waking moment had to be used productively in order to feel they had committed to their families and employees. Over time, this hard-working guilt cycle created bitterness.

Some employees would see their efforts and try to work just as hard. Time after time, any employee who tried to match them in pace would get burnt out and quit because they weren't valued for their efforts. An mentality of, "I'm working harder than you. Why should you be recognized?" was the subtle elephant in the room. Adding more work to competent people's plates without pay raises or acknowledgement bred animosity and bitterness in those employees.

Other employees would take advantage of their problem-solving work ethic by asking them to solve any problem they were faced with, never wanting to make a decision without their consent. Ultimately, this resulted in a high turnover rate, lower profit margins, and the partners being left to work even harder to hire and train new staff to replace their most competent workers.

Are you always sacrificing your time to help other people and just not getting the same amount of dedication back? Here are some truths about this:

- Your business is not God.
- Guilting yourself and others into working harder leads to frustration and bitterness.
- Business is not worth dying over.
- No one will ever care more about what you do in your business as much as God does.
- If your business is in a constant state of emergency, there is something seriously wrong.
- If you expect to get out what you put in, you're working for your gain and not God's.

I titled this chapter section the Woes of the Business Martyr because this is ultimately what many people choose to lay their lives down for. As a business owner, you should not be laying your whole life down for any business, ever. This is, in essence, idolatry. God has some pretty harsh things to say about idolatry.

Exodus 20:3-6

3 "You shall have no other gods before Me. 4 "You shall not make for yourself an idol, or any likeness of what is in heaven above or on the earth beneath or in the water under the earth. 5 You shall not worship them or serve them; for I, the Lord your God, am a jealous God, visiting the iniquity of the fathers on the children, on the third and the fourth generations of those who hate Me, 6 but showing lovingkindness to thousands, to those who love Me and keep My commandments.

Psalm 16:4

4 The sorrows of those who have bartered for another god will be multiplied; I shall not pour out their drink offerings of blood, Nor will I take their names upon my lips.

Galatians 5:19-20

19 Now the deeds of the flesh are evident, which are: immorality, impurity, sensuality, 20 idolatry, sorcery, enmities, strife, jealousy, outbursts of anger, disputes, dissensions, factions,

In just these three passages, we find that those who sin in idolatry will have punishment inflicted on their family to the third and fourth generation, and their sorrows shall multiply. Galatians goes on to say that they will not inherit the kingdom of God in the verses following. I could go on, but I hope you get the point. God will not share His glory with another (Isaiah 42:8).

When we are discussing idolatry, it's also good to recognize those that think they themselves are God. Do you know who else liked to praise himself instead of God? Here's a hint. He had a palace, praised himself for all the things he had built in his kingdom, and you can find him in the book of Daniel (chapter four). The answer is Nebuchadnezzar. God turned him into a beast for seven seasons.

You are not the savior of your business; God is. To think you can do this all on your own, to keep taking on more and more work, or to shoulder all these burdens without God is to try to become your own savior. This is a desecration to the gospel.

Acts 4:11-12

11 He is the stone which was rejected by you, the builders, but which became the chief corner stone. 12 And there is salvation in no one else; for there is no other name under heaven that has been given among men by which we must be saved."

If you make changes to put God first, He will honor it. Many of the issues your business is facing can be solved through accountability, delegation, compensation, technology, or even a healthy office culture! God calls us to be followers of Christ first and foremost because He has already prepared the good works we are supposed to be doing. We just need to walk in them!

Ephesians 2:8-10

8 For by grace you have been saved through faith; and that not of yourselves, it is the gift of God; 9 not as a result of works, so that no one may boast. 10 For we are His workmanship, created in Christ Jesus for good works, which God prepared beforehand so that we would walk in them.

Asking yourself some of these questions can help you understand what you are valuing in your business currently and what is the center of your work.

- Is the work I am doing pointing to God's glory, mine, or the business' glory?
- Am I afraid to put God first because it would mean letting go of my control?
- Is my dedication to my business inhibiting me from my dedication to God?
- Is my business distracting me from the transforming work that God is trying to do in my heart?
- Is my business causing me to be a poor example to my family of who a Christ follower should be?
- Am I perpetuating my ideas (or someone else's) of Christianity without regularly dissecting them against the word of God **in full context** on my own?
- When is the last time I gave my full and undivided attention to prayer, repentance, thanksgiving, praise, and worship **without giving myself a time limit?**

If answering any of these questions today is causing you to see issues or potential ones in your own heart, you need to immediately go before God in prayer and repentance. Ask God to help you. Confess your sin to Him. Even if it means you need to get up out of your office and sit in your car. Go do it. Delayed responses will only perpetuate your justification, projection, and avoidance. God cares more about your heart than your business. To put this off will end in regret and will have long term negative impacts to yourself and those around you.

Today:

- Ask God to help you put Him first in your business.
- Ask Him to take control of it, and run it His way.
- Thank God that His timing and plan is better than ours.
- Praise Him for caring more about your business and employees than you ever could.
- Ask Him to call you out when idolatry starts creeping into your life.
- Pray that the Lord would provide accountability partners to your life.

DAY 10

The Values We Hold

When I was a freshman in college, there was a marketing class scheduled to go to New York to tour agencies and learn about the different facets of marketing. There was one problem: the trip cost an extra $1,500 not included in tuition. I had no idea how I was going to pay for this. I decided that if God wanted me to go, He was going to have to pay for it.

A few weeks before the class, I looked in my student account to see someone had put money on my account! I called my parents to ask if it had been them, and they said, no. To this day, I have no idea who did that!

In New York, I read many books and fell into a love for David Ogilvy's marketing genius and a strong dislike for parts of his personality. We toured some of the largest agencies in the city. Now, every time I see the Trump Tower on television, I remember what it actually looks like on the inside!

In my memory, the lady that was assigned to be our tour guide for the agencies of we visited was equivalent to the exact likeness of Duchess Kate Middleton.[14] She was delightful. In transit to and from different agencies, she asked me what I wanted to do when I graduated.

"Well, I have to be careful what I choose, because I know that I'm extremely passionate. Whatever I put my mind to, I'll put my whole heart in it and go full speed. So, it has to be worth it."

I remember exactly where I was, at the bottom of a subway escalator, frozen in a moment. I was shocked at my own statement! How did I already know this about myself?! Where did this thought come from?

The next two years taught me that what I was describing was "The Alignment of Values." When you choose to do something, in order to truly feel successful, it has to be in alignment with your own personal values. Working for and with people who have the same values bonds you with a strength that is not easily shaken. As a business owner, you need to have clear business values that you and your team adhere to.

In order for values to ring true to us, they must be on paper, visible for everyone and reviewed regularly. Why? Because it doesn't become a reality if we aren't practicing them. God knew this when He was leading the Israelites.

Deuteronomy 11:13-21

> *13 "It shall come about, if you listen obediently to my commandments which I am commanding you today, to love the Lord your God and to serve Him with all your heart and all your soul, 14 that He will give the rain for your land in its season, the early and late rain, that you may gather in your grain and your new wine and your oil. 15 He will give grass in your fields for your cattle,*

---

[14] To this day, I cannot remember what her name is! Fact checking the likeness to Kate Middleton is, unfortunately, out of the question at this point.

*and you will eat and be satisfied. **16** Beware that your hearts are not deceived, and that you do not turn away and serve other gods and worship them. **17** Or the anger of the Lord will be kindled against you, and He will shut up the heavens so that there will be no rain and the ground will not yield its fruit; and you will perish quickly from the good land which the Lord is giving you.*

***18** "You shall therefore impress these words of mine on your heart and on your soul; and you shall bind them as a sign on your hand, and they shall be as frontals on your forehead. **19** You shall teach them to your sons, talking of them when you sit in your house and when you walk along the road and when you lie down and when you rise up. **20** You shall write them on the doorposts of your house and on your gates, **21** so that your days and the days of your sons may be multiplied on the land which the Lord swore to your fathers to give them, as long as the heavens remain above the earth.*

God tells them to obey Him. In order to help them from being deceived, He tells them to put His words everywhere and talk about them all the time. Your Biblical values need to be reflected in your business because it can be easy to forget what is guiding you. Many biblical values are actually held by people who are not Christians. This is because they make good business sense! Respect, The Golden Rule, Honesty, Faithfulness, Serving Others, etc. These are all largely values the world agrees are good in business. By surrounding yourself with people who commit to the same values, you help the focus of your business remain consistent.

God knows that in every aspect of our life, we have to be focused on Him.

Matthew 6:19-24

*   **19** *"Do not store up for yourselves treasures on earth, where moth and rust destroy, and where thieves break in and steal. **20** But store up for yourselves treasures in heaven, where neither moth nor rust destroys, and where thieves do not break in or steal; **21** for where your treasure is, there your heart will*

be also. 22 "The eye is the lamp of the body; so then if your eye is clear, your whole body will be full of light. 23 But if your eye is bad, your whole body will be full of darkness. If then the light that is in you is darkness, how great is the darkness! 24 "No one can serve two masters; for either he will hate the one and love the other, or he will be devoted to one and despise the other. You cannot serve God and wealth.

A common pitfall for many businesses is to solely focus on the profit. If your purpose is to obey God instead of the money, everything comes into alignment much easier! As you are seeking to build your business up in the Lord, take time today to ask God to help you understand what values you need to define in your business in order to run it accordingly.

Today:
- Thank God that He reveals to us the areas that He can be most glorified through what our businesses bring to the world.
- Ask God to show you what makes your business valuable to those around you and what standards He wants you to set in order to serve others well.
- Pray that God would reveal to you the places you can share these values and review them regularly within your business.
- Thank God that He can help us define what these values look like as they are acted out.
- Pray that He would help you hold yourself and others within your business accountable to these values daily.
- Repent of the ways you have acted that are not in alignment with the values He has called you to represent.
- Praise God for the Holy Spirit's leading in our life to convict us when we are not acting out the business values He has called us into.

DAY 11

Your Leadership Role

This is somewhat of a snore worthy topic for me. I've read quite a few books on leadership, Christian leadership, business leadership, servant leadership, yada, yada, yada. Here's what I hate about leadership books: They basically try to tell you to be an encouragement, positive, giving, loving, caring, self-sacrificing, whatever else people think is what makes a good leader. Most books on leadership are all head knowledge.

The thing is, leadership can only really be learned through actually practicing it in real life.

Here's one Example:

In Theory: When you have an issue, you should sit down with your employee, use the sandwich technique of good thing, bad thing, good thing, and coach your employee through becoming a better worker.

In Actuality: You have a manager screaming at a crying employee who now wants to go home, and you have a flood of customers at the counter waiting for someone to ring up their purchases.

The "sandwich technique" (start with praise, address item of needed improvement, and end with praise) is gone, and you're stuck wondering if you should fire someone, let someone go home, or convince everyone to stay and work together so you're not stuck doing everything by yourself with angry customers!

Okay, so that was extreme. Your leadership "techniques" and decisions will be different depending on the situation and your personality, but what I've learned from the Bible is that **leadership always comes down to setting an example.**

What does the Bible say about leadership? First, I think it is good to review how God viewed people who were in positions of leadership in the Old Testament. The kings of Israel give us a good starting point.

When it comes to leadership, many of us think the biggest part of leadership is wisdom. When we look at the life of Solomon, however, we find this not to be the case! Solomon is known as the wisest king in all of history, but the end of his life was actually a dud! Why? Because though he knew the clear commands that God had given him, he chose to go the opposite direction.

1 Kings 11:1-6

> *1 Now King Solomon loved many foreign women along with the daughter of Pharaoh: Moabite, Ammonite, Edomite, Sidonian, and Hittite women, 2 from the nations concerning which the Lord had said to the sons of Israel, "You shall not associate with them, nor shall they associate with you, for they will surely turn your heart away after their gods." Solomon held fast to these in love. 3 He had seven hundred wives, princesses, and three hundred concubines, and his wives turned his heart away. 4 For when Solomon was old, his wives turned his heart away after other gods; and his heart was not wholly devoted to the Lord his God, as the heart of David his father had been.*

5 For Solomon went after Ashtoreth the goddess of the Sidonians and after Milcom the detestable idol of the Ammonites. 6 Solomon did what was evil in the sight of the Lord, and did not follow the Lord fully, as David his father had done.

If you think Tiger Woods had a problem, we have soon forgotten Solomon. Not only were women his weakness, they turned his heart away from the Lord. If we keep reading in chapter 11, we find God telling Solomon how ticked off He is with him.

1 Kings 11:11-13

11 So the Lord said to Solomon, "Because you have done this, and you have not kept My covenant and My statutes, which I have commanded you, I will surely tear the kingdom from you, and will give it to your servant. 12 Nevertheless I will not do it in your days for the sake of your father David, but I will tear it out of the hand of your son. 13 However, I will not tear away all the kingdom, but I will give one tribe to your son for the sake of My servant David and for the sake of Jerusalem which I have chosen."

At this point, we find God has way more power than we ever could to discipline the manager of His people. God raises up external problems for Solomon (1 Kings 11).

Solomon finds a great guy to be the foreman of his building crew, Jeroboam. Jeroboam is said to be an industrious person, who's just doing his job. In verses 29-40, however, God has a prophet named Ahijah basically alter his entire life's existence.

1 Kings 11:29-33 & 37-40

29 It came about at that time, when Jeroboam went out of Jerusalem, that the prophet Ahijah the Shilonite found him on the road. Now Ahijah had clothed himself with a new cloak; and both of them were alone in the field. 30 Then Ahijah took hold of the new cloak which was on him and tore it into twelve pieces. 31 He said to Jeroboam, "Take for yourself ten pieces; for thus says

the Lord, the God of Israel, 'Behold, I will tear the kingdom out of the hand of
Solomon and give you ten tribes 32 (but he will have one tribe, for the sake of
My servant David and for the sake of Jerusalem, the city which I have chosen
from all the tribes of Israel), 33 because they have forsaken Me, and have
worshiped Ashtoreth the goddess of the Sidonians, Chemosh the god of Moab,
and Milcom the god of the sons of Ammon; and they have not walked in My
ways, doing what is right in My sight and observing My statutes and My
ordinances, as his father David did...37 I will take you, and you shall reign
over whatever you desire, and you shall be king over Israel. 38 Then it will
be, that if you listen to all that I command you and walk in My ways, and do
what is right in My sight by observing My statutes and My commandments, as
My servant David did, then I will be with you and build you an enduring
house as I built for David, and I will give Israel to you. 39 Thus I will afflict
the descendants of David for this, but not always.'" 40 Solomon sought
therefore to put Jeroboam to death; but Jeroboam arose and fled to Egypt to
Shishak king of Egypt, and he was in Egypt until the death of Solomon.

I'm sure after this run in with the prophet, Ahijah, Jeroboam is freaking out. Looking back on the Saul and David drama, we know that Solomon will probably want him dead. People are going to start trying to kill him. So, he runs for his life to Egypt, and doesn't come back till Solomon is dead.[15] At this point, the new kid in charge of Israel makes a poor move to increase taxes and everyone rebels, except Judah, to follow Jeroboam as their new king (1 Kings 12).

You may be thinking, "Well, God didn't punish Solomon in his lifetime, so it wasn't true

---

[15] Is anyone else noticing a running to Egypt for safety pattern? I mean, Mary and Joseph did it too! I feel like the Egyptian tourism bureau should be capitalizing on this, "Escape to Egypt, Remember Your Vacation for Centuries."

justice."

In this culture, however, your lineage is basically the pride and joy of your existence. To fail to leave a strong family line is to bring shame on your family and yourself. It's basically the biggest insult you can give someone to cut off their family line.

The thing I want to point out here is that God gives Jeroboam the same run down as Solomon, "if you will listen to all that I command you, and will walk in my ways, and do what is right in my eyes by keeping my statutes and my commandments, as David my servant did, I will be with you and will build you a sure house."

We keep reading to learn Jeroboam quickly fails at this job, and gets the kingdom removed from him as well! If we read the entire two books of 1st and 2nd Kings, we find the writer consistently points to one specific summary statement for each king. He always says, "He did evil in the sight of the Lord" or "He did what was right in the sight of the Lord."

That is, in essence, what God was looking for in every single one of these leaders. He tries to remind them by sending Elisha and Elijah the prophets to give them some hard confrontations.[16] He didn't care about their qualifications or natural abilities, all He wanted was for them to follow His commands!

Obedience note: Following God's commands also meant making sure the entire kingdom was following God's commands. The writer does note times when a king tries to honor God, but fails to take down the high places for sacrificing to other gods. Passive responses to the command of God are still as much a sin as doing the opposite of God's commands.

---

[16] Can you image how insanely hard it would be to be a prophet? Always telling people the sheer facts of their sin before God and people disliking you because of it doesn't sound like an enjoyable time to me at all!

So, if we know that all the kings in the Old Testament show a stark contrast to the perfect kingship of Jesus Christ, how exactly are we supposed to look at leadership and our failures as leaders? We will practice true leadership when we follow the example of Jesus. The New Testament repeatedly tells us this.

Hebrews 13:7-8

7 Remember those who led you, who spoke the word of God to you; and considering the result of their conduct, imitate their faith. 8 Jesus Christ is the same yesterday and today and forever.

Philippians 3:14-17

14 I press on toward the goal for the prize of the upward call of God in Christ Jesus. 15 Let us therefore, as many as are perfect, have this attitude; and if in anything you have a different attitude, God will reveal that also to you; 16 however, let us keep living by that same standard to which we have attained. 17 Brethren, join in following my example, and observe those who walk according to the pattern you have in us.

1 Peter 2:20-21

20 For what credit is there if, when you sin and are harshly treated, you endure it with patience? But if when you do what is right and suffer for it you patiently endure it, this finds favor with God. 21 For you have been called for this purpose, since Christ also suffered for you, leaving you an example for you to follow in His steps,

1 Peter 5:1-4

1 Therefore, I exhort the elders among you, as your fellow elder and witness of the sufferings of Christ, and a partaker also of the glory that is to be revealed, 2 shepherd the flock of God among you, exercising oversight not under compulsion, but voluntarily, according to the will of God; and not for sordid gain, but with eagerness; 3 nor yet as lording it over those allotted to your charge, but proving to be examples to the flock. 4 And when the Chief Shepherd appears, you will receive the unfading crown of glory.

In 9th grade, I heard a youth summer camp speaker summarize this nicely, "If you really want to be a leader, follow after Jesus with your whole heart. One day, you'll look behind you and see a whole line of people following you."

In essence, good leaders are first and foremost, followers.

Though some leadership books may have good points, the focus many times isn't in the right place. The focus in these books is often on exemplifying special characteristics or formulas to bring about good leadership. Our focus instead should be about living your life for Christ. Once you do that, all of the amiable leadership qualities necessary become a byproduct of your pursuit of Christ.

Today:
- Pray that God would help you follow the example of Christ's life.
- Ask Him to show you how you can imitate the love of Christ and the fruits of the spirit in your personal life and your professional one.
- Ask God to show you the areas of your heart that are keeping you from following Christ's leadership example.
- Ask Him to show you how others are watching your actions and interpreting who Christ is through them.
- Pray that others would see a true reflection of Jesus in your life.
- Ask God to teach you how to follow Jesus' actions and share His heart for those around you.

DAY 12

Putting Off God's Calling

I am going to start out by saying this bluntly: God will get your attention one way or another.

Have you ever found yourself avoiding God because you are scared of what He's going to say? From personal experience, I would recommend you make the time to work through that before He forces you to make the time. God has a way of getting our attention in ways we wouldn't have picked.

I have seen this to be the case time and time again, when those who follow Jesus refuse to listen to what He's calling them to do. For me, God wanted my attention in writing this book. When the suggestion first crossed my mind, I thought, *"No, that would be too 'pushy.' People don't want to know I'm a Christian, they just want to know I'm good at my job."*

A month later, I was reading an entrepreneurial book, and there was this section on how you must be open to spirituality. The writer then suggested a good business shaman that can hear from the dead and coach your business through reading your team's aura.

God poked my heart and said, "People are already seeking spiritual guidance on how to run their business, and are being directed away from Me."

The next shocker for me was that this shaman was conducting spiritual retreats in different parts of the world, one of the places included where I live!

I started praying. *God, I am not spiritually qualified to do this kind of project. Also, I didn't have time to do this type of project. This might be a good idea, but a pipe dream for the future.*[17]

Within the span of three days, all of my clients told me that they were so busy, they didn't have time to meet with me this month. I was stunned. As I looked at my calendar, I felt as if God smugly said, "Look at all the free time you have to write this book!"

"Touché, God. You have me there."

I am desperately warning you against putting off the call of God in your life, because I have seen all too often where it leads. God usually starts telling you where He's calling you with the conviction of the Holy Spirit.

Refusing to listen to the Holy Spirit is something that people get better at the more they do it. For those people, God getting your attention might be more gradual as you keep sliding away from Him. In some cases, it isn't noticeable for years, but when it finally hits you, I pray there is a way to avoid permanent damage. One person that comes to mind from the Bible who tried to put off God's call is Jonah.

---

[17] For the record, I have about 80 good ideas a day. Filtering is a necessary habit for me.

Jonah 1:1-3

> *1 The word of the Lord came to Jonah the son of Amittai saying, 2 "Arise, go to Nineveh the great city and cry against it, for their wickedness has come up before Me." 3 But Jonah rose up to flee to Tarshish from the presence of the Lord. So he went down to Joppa, found a ship which was going to Tarshish, paid the fare and went down into it to go with them to Tarshish from the presence of the Lord.*

Jonah hears from God, and legitimately runs away. When I looked up the locations of these two cities, I just started laughing. Tarshish is located in what is modern day southern Spain. Nineveh is located in northern Iraq. I can just imagine Jonah's thought process. *European holiday on the beach or roasting in the desert with some Assyrians who make wallpaper out of human flesh? I've always loved the beach. I should book my trip, and leave so God knows my schedule is full.*

I'm sure God just sighed as he watched Jonah slink onto that ship and hide below deck for a nap, hoping God wouldn't see him.[18] God sends a storm that is so bad, the sailors are starting to throw things overboard. They find Jonah in the hull and tell him to wake up and pray to his God for their lives. It's interesting that they actually have a culture that believes in a higher power, because they all decided to cast lots to see who messed with a spiritual being.

Jonah 1:7-9

> *7 Each man said to his mate, "Come, let us cast lots so we may learn on whose account this calamity has struck us." So they cast lots and the lot fell on Jonah. 8 Then they said to him, "Tell us, now! On whose account has this*

---

[18] Stubborn and an insanely hard sleeper? Seems like an interesting combination. Just goes to show you that some people can sleep well while blatantly disobeying the Lord.

calamity struck us? What is your occupation? And where do you come from? What is your country? From what people are you?" **9** *He said to them, "I am a Hebrew, and I fear the Lord God of heaven who made the sea and the dry land."*

The first two questions they ask Jonah are, "Who is doing this to us, and what do you do for a living?"

I love that! They want to know what exactly this guy is doing in his professional life that would make God so angry. *What are you a professional hitman?!* Jonah ends up telling them who he is, and suggests they throw him overboard to save themselves.

Jonah 1:12-13

12 *He said to them, "Pick me up and throw me into the sea. Then the sea will become calm for you, for I know that on account of me this great storm has come upon you."* **13** *However, the men rowed desperately to return to land but they could not, for the sea was becoming even stormier against them.*

When we refuse to obey God in the business He has for us, it has huge impacts on the people around us. Jonah was basically telling these men to kill him in order to save themselves. Their response was to ignore his suggestion and just work harder. In the end, they realized that their only hope was to listen to his advice, but they ask God for a pardon on their actions.

Jonah 1:14-16

14 *Then they called on the Lord and said, "We earnestly pray, O Lord, do not let us perish on account of this man's life and do not put innocent blood on us; for You, O Lord, have done as You have pleased."* **15** *So they picked up Jonah, threw him into the sea, and the sea stopped its raging.* **16** *Then the men feared the Lord greatly, and they offered a sacrifice to the Lord and made vows.*

The sea immediately calms, when Jonah is thrown into the water. For these men, their lives have been intensely altered with their first-hand encounter of Jonah's disobedience before a holy God. If I were them, I would be fearing the Lord right about then too! So, what happens next? God sends a fish to swallow Jonah. This is what gets me! He's there for 3 days and 3 nights! I can't even sit in an ice house for more than 4 hours with fish! He's in there for 72 hours before he finally decides to repent!

Jonah 2:7-10

> 7 *"While I was fainting away, I remembered the Lord, And my prayer came to You, Into Your holy temple. 8 "Those who regard vain idols Forsake their faithfulness, 9 But I will sacrifice to You With the voice of thanksgiving. That which I have vowed I will pay. Salvation is from the Lord."*

Jonah finally agrees to apologize to God, and God has the fish vomit him up.[19] Here is where God again gives him the same command. This time, Jonah goes, tells the people God's warning, and they have a city-wide repentance, asking for God's forgiveness. Because Jonah was obedient, 120,000 people were saved from the wrath of God!

Repenting in the midst of God's punishment isn't the end of God's call to us for obedience. God didn't let Jonah off the hook.[20] We still need to follow through on what He has told us to do. God also doesn't want part of our efforts in following His call. He wants all of it. Everything needs to be on the table when committing to where He is calling us.

Refusing to follow through on God's call to you in business can have a serious impact on the people around you. David Green knew this to be true when he felt God call him to close his Hobby Lobby retail stores on Sundays. People told him that if God called him to do it, God would honor his commitment.

---

[19] I'm realizing that salvation isn't always as romantic as Paul's description of the bride of Christ. God is still romantic, but Jonah must have smelled putrid.

[20] Pun intended #cantstopwontstop

He started closing stores across the nation, and the numbers started dropping. It wasn't until he converted the final stores to close on Sundays that they started to see their financials go back up again![21]

Today:

- Pray and ask God to help you keep your heart open to what He is calling you to do.
- Ask God for the faith and endurance to commit everything to Him when He calls you to act.
- Ask God to show you if there is anything in your life that you are not allowing Him to lead.
- Praise God and thank Him for using us in part of His plan to reach the world.
- Praise God that He forgives us when we make mistakes.
- Praise God for how awesome He is in being able to display His holiness and salvation to others even when we are sinning.
- Pray that you will have discernment in hearing God's leading.

---

[21] Right Now Media. (2015). The Hobby Lobby Decision [Video]. Retrieved from https://www.rightnowmedia.org/

DAY 13

Bitterness

One day, I was at work, and I was angry. This is always a bad spot to be for me because I am a verbal processor. Desk mates be wary. This is a day to work from home because without my prayer journal handy, I can easily become a raging cannon of aimless shots towards any moving civilian. This, however, was not the first day of being angry. I had been angry for at least a month. In the last few weeks, it had just started to become visible to everyone instead of the select few I had expressed myself to.

For all of you internal processors, the worst thing you can do to an external processor is to ask them to keep it all inside. This was a moment in my life when I had a very small timeframe to express all of my emotions to my husband, in the privacy of our own room, and he would desperately try not to fall asleep while I was talking.[22]

---

[22] I believe the best ideas come to me between 10:30-11:00pm. That's about an hour after my husband falls asleep. This is the point in my day when I silently pump my fists in victory and text him what he missed, so he can read it in the morning while my brain is on reboot. When I'm too excited, I wake him up. Those are the days he thinks the house is on fire...I digress.

On this particular angry day, I had had enough. I realized that this had turned into something worse than anger; it was bitterness. Anger is short lived, but bitterness eats at you continually with stewing poison. I knew the data on bitterness and how it has long term effects on your health, energy, fulfillment, and success.[23] I knew I had to get rid of it!

At lunch time, I Googled what the Bible has to say about bitterness. A 5-minute sermon clip by John Piper popped up, so I decided to listen to it. That man nailed me to the wall in truthful confrontation. The scripture he started off with was talking about revenge.

Romans 12:19

> *19 Never take your own revenge, beloved, but leave room for the wrath of God, for it is written, "Vengeance is Mine, I will repay," says the Lord.*

He then walked through how having this bitterness towards someone else means you wish them to receive punishment or justice to account for their actions. Vengeance is not our job!

The next punch to the stomach he threw at me was that to live in bitterness is to believe that God's punishment of hell is not enough of a punishment for that person's sins. This isn't something we should ever wish on anyone in light of the saving grace of Jesus Christ and God's heart for reconciliation.

The final blow he took me out with was this: To live in bitterness towards someone who is a follower of Christ is to believe that Christ's sacrifice on the cross was not enough to cover their sins or mine.

---

[23] Okay, I know this is nerdy, but conviction through data is actually a pretty common way God moves my heart.

He said, "If they're in hell, you don't need to add to their punishment. If their load was borne and forgiven and paid at the cross, you would dishonor the Lord if you didn't share in the forgiveness."[24]

At this point, I was mentally laying on the ground, dazed. We are all sinners in need of a perfect savior. If we do not believe Jesus's sacrifice was big enough to pay for their sins, it was not big enough to pay for ours. We are therefore left with no hope in this life.

So, how do we overcome this negative mental cycle? Piper was very clear to say that you have to bring it to the cross. So, that's what I started to do. Every time I would think about what made me upset, I would remind myself. *Christ has already paid for this! Leave it on the cross for Him to cover.*

It took me a few weeks, but within a month, I was finally able to start feeling normal! I was finally able to have joyful moments that weren't shrouded by darkness or poisoned by discoloration. When it finally came time for me to confront the issues that had occurred, I was able to look straight into the faces of people that had hurt me and only see those Christ died for. I left that meeting feeling like a miracle of God had just happened. It was freeing and incredible. I felt no anger. God is so good.

Do you know who else had a problem with bitterness? Jonah! Didn't think we were going to hit the whole book, did you?! Here the man has finally obeyed God, and was indignant at God's response to the repentant hearts of the Ninevites! He basically says, "I knew this would happen!"

---

[24] Desiring God. (2018). How to Battle Bitterness [Video]. Retrieved from https://www.desiringgod.org/messages/the-word-of-god-is-at-work-in-you/excerpts/how-to-battle-bitterness

Jonah 4:2

2 He prayed to the Lord and said, "Please Lord, was not this what I said while I was still in my own country? Therefore in order to forestall this I fled to Tarshish, for I knew that You are a gracious and compassionate God, slow to anger and abundant in lovingkindness, and one who relents concerning calamity.

Jonah clearly did not like the people of Nineveh. He knew in his heart that if he told them to repent before God and they did, God would forgive them! Jonah wanted no part in God's forgiveness towards them! Jonah says he would rather die than live through God's forgiveness towards these people. He sulks up a hill outside the city to watch and see if God will change his mind. Maybe he's thinking Sodom and Gomorrah is about to repeat itself.[25] He's not about to miss fire from heaven.[26]

So, he starts prepping. Just like that blanket fort you really didn't want in the middle of your living room before company comes, he builds himself a little shelter. God even lets a plant grow and gives him additional shade. Talk about pitching in for boojie![27] This is where God tries to make a point. He causes a worm to eat the plant the next day so it wilts. Then He sends a hot blistering wind to add to the heat of the day. Jonah is equivalent to a child who's been looking forward to Netflix all day when the WIFI cuts out.

---

[25] Actually, Nineveh was located on a major fault line and had some decent documented earth quakes in the past, so I'm assuming this would have been more likely. Years later, however, the entire city gets destroyed like the prophet Amos predicted it would be (through a civil war that levels most of the city and makes it forgotten to people for centuries).

[26] Although, seeing Sodom and Gomorrah's destruction and turning to a pillar of salt doesn't really sound like it worked out the first time for Lot's wife.

[27] For you older generations, this means posh or fancy. Add that to your next board meeting!

Jonah 4:8b-11

> *8b he became faint and begged with all his soul to die, saying, "Death is better to me than life." 9 Then God said to Jonah, "Do you have good reason to be angry about the plant?" And he said, "I have good reason to be angry, even to death." 10 Then the Lord said, "You had compassion on the plant for which you did not work and which you did not cause to grow, which came up overnight and perished overnight. 11 Should I not have compassion on Nineveh, the great city in which there are more than 120,000 persons who do not know the difference between their right and left hand, as well as many animals?"*

I don't know about you, but God setting me up to be an object lesson isn't always my idea of a good time. He looks right at the anger Jonah has and basically says, "You care about this plant, that you didn't work for, so much that you'd die over it? Why shouldn't I care about 120,000 people who weren't taught right from wrong, but still repented?"

The book ends with God's proverbial mic drop.

Bitterness tends to focus on small stupid things like Jonah did, and makes us mad at God about big things He is choosing to "let happen." Regardless of the reason, we are never justified in being angry with God for His mercy. Jonah had spent a lot of time getting to know God before this moment. He even says, "for I knew that you are a gracious God and merciful, slow to anger and abounding in steadfast love, and relenting from disaster."

God's personality had not changed. Jonah knew He was a good God. He just didn't agree with the way God chose to love. Why are we becoming enemies of God over His complete justice and mercy? If we're not okay with His ultimate ability to judge the world and give grace, why are we okay with it in our own lives?[28] Bitterness should not be welcome in your

---

[28] Hint! No, actually, answer! It's because we're sinners and selfish.

heart or in your business. God has never changed. Bitterness should not be changing your attitude and work habits.

Today:

- Praise God that He chooses to show you mercy and grace through Jesus Christ even though you were a wretched sinner.
- Ask God to help you deal with the bitterness you may have in your heart for others in your life.
- Continually remind yourself to take those poisonous thoughts to the cross where Christ paid for all sins.
- Pray that God would stir your heart to pray for those that have hurt you.
- Whether they are lost, in need of a Savior, or redeemed by Christ's sacrifice, praise God that His justice is fully perfect and you are not responsible to contribute to it.

DAY 14

When You Want to Give Up

When my husband and I first were engaged, we struggled to communicate effectively with one another. I grew up with six siblings, all of which talk at the same time to be heard. We would openly yell at each other across the table to get people's attention during dinner, and are, in general, very loud people. In my childhood, the dinner table had fights, people being sent to their room, crying, food being stolen while others weren't looking, things being flicked across the table at you "by accident," sudden bursts of song, rants, and debates. The two rules I remember we had to seriously follow were that you had to be clothed in order to eat, and you had to save food for dad. Everything else was open for discussion, regularly.

This was a culture shock to my husband. My husband's family only raises their voices when they are irate. They are all passionate about the truth, but challenge people through calm dialogue and questioning. Whenever we would get into a discussion, and I wanted to prove a point, my voice would get louder. To him, I was yelling, and he would be overwhelmed. Suddenly he'd start crying, because he thought I was at the point of no return. He thought I was about to call off our engagement.

To me, crying was what my family only did when you had no other options or arguments left. I only cry when I feel I am defeated or have nothing else left to do. As soon as he started crying, I assumed he couldn't handle the discussion anymore. I would get so mad that he was giving up the debate so easily! I would immediately lose respect for him and his ability to stand up for himself. After months, we finally realized our perceptions and backgrounds had impacted how we viewed the same situation. He had to understood that I wasn't furious, and I had to practice calming my voice down during discussion.[29]

Our backgrounds, previous experiences, and culture can all get in the way of our understanding. This happens a lot in our relationship with God. Sometimes we see where Jesus is, and in faith, we try to follow him. Part way through trusting Him, however, we remember what is logical, what has happened to others in the past, our previous experiences, how this could end differently, and we become afraid to move forward or give up all together. Peter had this issue when he saw Jesus walking on the water.

Matthew 14:22-33

> *22 Immediately He made the disciples get into the boat and go ahead of Him to the other side, while He sent the crowds away. 23 After He had sent the crowds away, He went up on the mountain by Himself to pray; and when it was evening, He was there alone. 24 But the boat was already a long distance from the land, battered by the waves; for the wind was contrary. 25 And in the fourth watch of the night He came to them, walking on the sea. 26 When the disciples saw Him walking on the sea, they were terrified, and said, "It is a ghost!" And they cried out in fear. 27 But immediately Jesus spoke to them,*

---

[29] Seriously, I distinctly remember a desire to not leave anyone out of conversation so strongly, that I used to talk loud enough at restaurants to make sure the people next to us could hear the whole story if it was a good one. Yes, I was that kid you probably laughed at in the car on your way home.

*saying, "Take courage, it is I; do not be afraid." **28** Peter said to Him, "Lord, if it is You, command me to come to You on the water." **29** And He said, "Come!" And Peter got out of the boat, and walked on the water and came toward Jesus. **30** But seeing the wind, he became frightened, and beginning to sink, he cried out, "Lord, save me!" **31** Immediately Jesus stretched out His hand and took hold of him, and said to him, "You of little faith, why did you doubt?" **32** When they got into the boat, the wind stopped. **33** And those who were in the boat worshiped Him, saying, "You are certainly God's Son!"*

The logic is that people don't walk on water, unless it's frozen. On top of that, they are in the middle of a serious struggle to make headway with their boat when they see this bodily form walking by. Mark 6 recounts this story a little differently.

Mark 6:48

48 Seeing them straining at the oars, for the wind was against them, at about the fourth watch of the night He came to them, walking on the sea; and He intended to pass by them.

Jesus was going to pass by them! He came by to check on them, but was about to keep going! He saw they were afraid, however, and stops to talk with them, "Don't be afraid, it is I."

In seeing Jesus do something incredible and wanting to be a part of it, Peter performs a test to confirm this was actually Jesus, "If it's really you, command me to come to you on the water." Jesus does and we see that at first, it's a good experience. Yes, this is Jesus. He called me to do this, and it's miraculously working out. Half way through however, he starts realizing that this is way scarier than he ever imagined it would be. He starts to sink.

In crying out for the Lord, Jesus reaches out and saves him. Here, the son of God is directly in front of him, he's seeing miraculous confirmation that this truly is God commanding him to come, and he still has doubt. Jesus even says, "Why did you doubt?"

If God called you this far into business, He did not leave you there to fend for yourself. As a matter of fact, He is already here waiting for you to reach out to Him. Sometimes we let financials, market changes, competition, or even our family life make us become afraid. We start to sink into fear, but why? If God has not given you clear direction to stop, why are you doubting His protection and provision?

A few months ago, I was defeated. I felt I had tried everything I could to help my business grow, and I was done trying. *Maybe I had misheard God. He wouldn't have made it this hard to follow Him.*[30] I had a long hard cry, and my dog tried to repeatedly comfort me by sticking his head in my face to make sure I was breathing. Through gasps for air that avoided getting his dog hair and wet nose in my mouth, I texted one of my business friends, and told her that I was giving up.

Her text back was short, "Business owners don't give up, they take breaks. Take the day off if you have to, but you're coming back to it on Monday."

It was harsh, insensitive, and the cold water I needed to get over myself.

The questions that kept coming into my head were, "Who owns the entire world and its resources? Who called you to start this business? Do you believe I am faithful? Who does the Bible say that I am?"

Gah! He just kept confronting this doubt and fear in me over and over again through His word. Then, I started thinking through the reality of my situation.

I had been looking at all the aspects around me that the world describes as success. I wasn't measuring up, at least not fast enough for what I thought I should be. As an achiever, who

---

[30] There is nothing in scripture that supports this statement. I'm just a baby, feeling sorry for myself.

loves data and benchmarks, I was comparing what I wanted my business to become to what I have right now. I was also missing the fact that most of the people I was measuring up against took a long time to get to where they are today!

The truth is, if God called you to business or gifted you to be good at it, He did not call you do it alone. God will always be there for us!

Hebrews 13:5-7

> *5 Make sure that your character is free from the love of money, being content with what you have; for He Himself has said, "I will never desert you, nor will I ever forsake you," 6 so that we confidently say, "The Lord is my helper, I will not be afraid. What will man do to me?" 7 Remember those who led you, who spoke the word of God to you; and considering the result of their conduct, imitate their faith.*

We already touched on verse 7 of Hebrews 13, in imitating others who follow Christ to become a good leader, but when we look at it in the larger context of verses 5 and 6, it just gets better!

Here we see that writer of Hebrews knew the love of money is something many people struggle with. Why? Well, what do we know about money? It is used in exchange for goods and services and has an economically assigned value accepted by society. Does that make it bad? No. Without it, we would resort to simply trading goods and services (which can be large and cumbersome for some of you). The **love** of money is bad. To love the value that money brings is bad.

This is because our value is supposed to come from Jesus. Money is what our culture perceives as a factor of success. What is ultimate success for a Christian? From day one, we learned it is to live a life that glorifies God. If we focus on what the world thinks is valuable, we will miss Jesus. If He will never leave us, there is nothing this earth can throw at us that God cannot handle. Why should we be afraid?

Even when we are blind to God's hand or are suffering through things that are difficult, God is still working. Taking a day off to pray has never been something I really enjoy doing. Mostly because it is mentally painful for me to feel that I'm not doing anything. This is a lie. It's like thinking bringing your car in for an oil change is a waste of time. You have to do it if you're going to preserve your vehicle.

You have to take breaks with God to become more efficient and to fight the lies of chaos around you. Every time I do it, it completely centers my focus, gives me clear direction for where I'm going next, and gives me actionable steps to get there. All of which I spend way too much time trying to figure out on my own. Without focusing on Jesus, I will sink in fear. Giving up isn't an option for me, and it isn't an option for you.

Can you imagine if Peter hadn't doubted? Three of the four gospel writers don't even take the time to document Peter's little episode. They only talked about Jesus walking on the water and immediately calming the storm by entering the boat.

What if everyone else got out of the boat to follow because they saw that Peter didn't have any issues trusting Lord to come through? Let's not forget that everyone else stayed in the boat! You as a business owner have already stepped out in faith much farther than most people do in their entire lifetime! Doing what you do and taking on these types of challenges is a unique skill set. No one else does it because it takes a lot of courage! Imagine how many people are going to see the work of God in your life when you persevere in trusting the Lord.

Today:
- Thank God for providing for you.
- Praise Him for never leaving you.
- Thank Him for giving you the opportunity to grow your faith in Him.
- Thank Him for never changing.
- Praise Him for being all powerful.
- Thank Him that you are not alone in your business.
- Pray that He would help you to remember who the Bible says He is.
- Pray that He would help you recall the times He has confirmed His direction on your life.

- Thank Him that He is in charge of your business.
- Pray that God would help you trust Him and focus on Him. Remember your personality and when you normally see this doubt start creeping up in your life, block off a day in advance to seek the Lord and realign yourself with His focus. If you're already at this point of doubt, you might need to take the day off today or this weekend.

DAY 15

Failed Observations, Outsider Perspectives, and Delegation

I've never liked running. It's probably because I was the 2-mile runner for every track and field meet in high school and it was so antisocial![31] I have a wonderful border collie, however, and that requires lots of exercise. In order to push myself and help my dog, I decided I needed accountability. I registered for a 5k race, and told my very frugal husband that we couldn't quit because we already paid for it! [32]

---

[31] My opinions have slightly changed on this topic recently. Running is way more fun when you can stop whenever you want and no one is judging you. All you have to say is, "Okay, go potty," and let your dog sniff something whenever you want to stop!

[32] This is also how you get a frugal person to go on vacations. "Surprise! You have to go, because it's already paid for!" I am not liable for your marital issues in this approach.

R . N . A N D E R S O N

My husband is so much faster than I am. He runs and circles a few extra blocks to meet back up with me whenever we run together. This used to bother me. I rediscovered the Planet Money podcast, however, and now I'm contently over it.

Because I need the extra speed, I always leash up my dog to a waist harness, which pulls me forward when he's excited. This particular 5k was set on a dirt road and portions of black top. In early March, we started training. It had just rained the day before, and this was the first real warm day of the spring.

On this particular day, my husband was far ahead of me. I was pushing so hard to just keep running, but my dog kept trying to run through every single puddle! When we finally got to the end, I was gasping, relieved, and he was filthy. I loaded him in the car, trying to avoid contact with my white fabric seats, and we headed for home.

Later that evening, I notice my dog was having trouble walking. I looked at his paws, and realized that I was the worst dog owner in the world. Every paw had giant blisters from getting burnt on the black top. I had no idea. I felt horrible! It was so bad, he wasn't allowed to run on any concrete for the next 4 months!

Many business owners start off like the solo runner. When we're in the middle of running, we rarely think to slow down to take the rocks out of our shoes, even though it would probably increase our speed. *I am aware of my own pain, but I can tough it out.*

When your business grows, you start leading other people such as customers and employees. This is like leading other runners or running with your dog. Sometimes the pace is so hard to keep up with, that you don't notice what's happening around you.

God is the ultimate manager. He always has a plan. I have never once seen God micromanage someone. God is never too busy for us when we seek His guidance. He has never broken a promise. He has never under delivered. He has never let anyone undermine His ultimate authority. He has never changed His expectations for us. He has never failed to serve ultimate justice and provide complete mercy. He knows exactly the intentions of everyone because He can see our hearts.

The reality is, we will never be the ultimate manager, because we are not God. We are going to mess up, but God still puts us in charge of things all the time to manage on His behalf. This actually happened to Moses. First God told him to talk to Pharaoh, then lead the people out of Egypt. In Exodus 18, we find him communicating with God and judging the people of Israel daily. His responsibilities have grown, but his time has not.

In this time period, we see the first documented occurrence of a grandparent's cross-country road trip to drop off the grandkids.[33]

Exodus 18:5-27

> *5 Then Jethro, Moses' father-in-law, came with his sons and his wife to Moses in the wilderness where he was camped, at the mount of God. 6 He sent word to Moses, "I, your father-in-law Jethro, am coming to you with your wife and her two sons with her." 7 Then Moses went out to meet his father-in-law, and he bowed down and kissed him; and they asked each other of their welfare and went into the tent. 8 Moses told his father-in-law all that the Lord had done to Pharaoh and to the Egyptians for Israel's sake, all the hardship that had befallen them on the journey, and how the Lord had delivered them. 9 Jethro rejoiced over all the goodness which the Lord had done to Israel, in delivering them from the hand of the Egyptians.*

> *10 So Jethro said, "Blessed be the Lord who delivered you from the hand of the Egyptians and from the hand of Pharaoh, and who delivered the people from under the hand of the Egyptians. 11 Now I know that the Lord is greater*

---

[33] Did anyone else just realize that Moses has been kid-less during most of his rise to management?

than all the gods; indeed, it was proven when they dealt proudly against the people." 12 Then Jethro, Moses' father-in-law, took a burnt offering and sacrifices for God, and Aaron came with all the elders of Israel to eat a meal with Moses' father-in-law before God.

13 It came about the next day that Moses sat to judge the people, and the people stood about Moses from the morning until the evening. 14 Now when Moses' father-in-law saw all that he was doing for the people, he said, "What is this thing that you are doing for the people? Why do you alone sit as judge and all the people stand about you from morning until evening?" 15 Moses said to his father-in-law, "Because the people come to me to inquire of God. 16 When they have a dispute, it comes to me, and I judge between a man and his neighbor and make known the statutes of God and His laws."

17 Moses' father-in-law said to him, "The thing that you are doing is not good. 18 You will surely wear out, both yourself and these people who are with you, for the task is too heavy for you; you cannot do it alone. 19 Now listen to me: I will give you counsel, and God be with you. You be the people's representative before God, and you bring the disputes to God, 20 then teach them the statutes and the laws, and make known to them the way in which they are to walk and the work they are to do. 21 Furthermore, you shall select out of all the people able men who fear God, men of truth, those who hate dishonest gain; and you shall place these over them as leaders of thousands, of hundreds, of fifties and of tens. 22 Let them judge the people at all times; and let it be that every major dispute they will bring to you, but every minor dispute they themselves will judge. So it will be easier for you, and they will bear the burden with you. 23 If you do this thing and God so commands you, then you will be able to endure, and all these people also will go to their place in peace."

24 So Moses listened to his father-in-law and did all that he had said. 25 Moses chose able men out of all Israel and made them heads over the people, leaders of thousands, of hundreds, of fifties and of tens. 26 They judged the people at all times; the difficult dispute they would bring to Moses, but every minor dispute they themselves would judge. 27 Then Moses bade his father-in-law farewell, and he went his way into his own land.

God will not tell you to fix every problem inside your business, but we learn the following concepts from Jethro's appearance in the book of Exodus:

- You can become blind to problems when you are living them every day.
- You are not sustainable for growth if you're doing everything by yourself.
- When we reflect on what God has brought us through, God can still be glorified, though we have failures.
- Everyone will appreciate it when you delegate responsibilities and only help with big issues because it's more efficient.
- Recommendations for change are sometimes taken best from those outside your day to day business.
- "We've always done it this way" is an observation not a solution.
- Consultants don't get hired on once they solve your problem, they go home.
- Moses had child care! (Okay, this last one was really just novel to me maybe.)

When you have management issues inside your business, you usually have a hard time putting your finger on the problem because you're living it every day. Sometimes we don't even realize we have a problem until we have someone outside observe what's going on. Businesses lose thousands of dollars over this regularly.

If you have employees, the odds are, people inside your business have already tried to point out that something is wrong. I'm assuming other people within the nation of Israel knew this judicial process was worse than getting tabs for their camels, but to change it hadn't been a direct command from God yet.

Is anyone else's mind blown by this one chapter? We know Jethro was a priest, but he had no idea that the Lord was the greatest God until he heard what Moses just went through. Jethro might not have had a full understanding of who God was until this moment, but he knew a thing or two about delegation.

I am guessing he wasn't the only one, but with a schedule like Moses,' who had time to talk to him? It's also a safe bet that the people of Israel were complaining a lot already, so Moses didn't regard hearing their opinions very highly. Thus far, they have freaked out about food and water. Now, they have to wait months for their legislative branch to do anything.

History has proven that hiring people for positions of leadership in swift waves can lead to a lot of confusion without set policies. So, God walks through the next twelve chapters of rules and temple standards to make sure the new leadership team and priests have something to guide their decisions. The rest of Exodus looks pretty similar to a God-organized on-boarding program.[34] A little dry, full of rules, but absolutely vital to the success of Israel surviving in the desert and worshiping a Holy God.

What exactly does this mean for us? Firstly, God doesn't have to be the one telling you each and every step to improve your business. Secondly, we need to be observant of how we are leading and its effects on the people around us. Thirdly, the sooner we ask for help, the faster things are going to improve.

Today:
- Read through Exodus eighteen again, and pray that God would highlight the areas that you need to improve in personally.
- Thank God for being your perfect manager.
- Ask God's help in observing the needs of those around you when they first arise.

---

[34] Which is all written down by the way! Moses didn't train every person one on one. Efficiency at its finest!

- Ask that God would put people in your life like Jethro who can cut through the everyday and show you how to become efficient and intentional with your time.
- Praise Him for teaching you continually.
- Pray for your employees and clients (current and future ones) that God would give them patience with you in your imperfections.
- Ask Him to grow you in the area of delegation.
- Ask His help in finding ways to simplify training and processes.

DAY 16

Not Everyone Will Like You

When I was in college, there was a time where I seriously struggled through how following Christ was possible. Many of my friends had started participating in activities that I wasn't sure could align with what the Bible taught.

I distinctly remember someone during this portion of my life say, "Following what the Bible says is impossible. There's no point in trying because you'll never be able to do it. You need to relax and stop worrying so much about what the Bible says."

I was so shrouded by people, who didn't want to hear anything about what the Bible had to say, that I started to wonder if that statement was the truth. My friends would visibly shut off when I brought up things that I was feeling conflicted over. I was struggling and in need of personal accountability, which no one seemed willing to help me with. Over a break from school, I came to realize that the questionable statement was *partially* right.

Following the Bible out of moral obligation or duty is incredibly difficult. If we look at some of the things the Bible calls us to do, it seems almost impossible. Here's part of Paul's letter to the church of Thessalonica.

1 Thessalonians 5:12-24

> *12 But we request of you, brethren, that you appreciate those who diligently labor among you, and have charge over you in the Lord and give you instruction, 13 and that you esteem them very highly in love because of their work. Live in peace with one another. 14 We urge you, brethren, admonish the unruly, encourage the fainthearted, help the weak, be patient with everyone. 15 See that no one repays another with evil for evil, but always seek after that which is good for one another and for all people. 16 Rejoice always; 17 pray without ceasing; 18 in everything give thanks; for this is God's will for you in Christ Jesus. 19 Do not quench the Spirit; 20 do not despise prophetic utterances. 21 But examine everything carefully; hold fast to that which is good; 22 abstain from every form of evil.*
>
> *23 Now may the God of peace Himself sanctify you entirely; and may your spirit and soul and body be preserved complete, without blame at the coming of our Lord Jesus Christ. 24 Faithful is He who calls you, and He also will bring it to pass.*

Let's dig into these passages a bit more. I wanted to make a bullet list of the directions Paul gives in 1 Thessalonians because sometimes it can be easier to see in a checklist. We are to do the following:

- Show appreciation for those who are spiritually leading us
- Live peacefully
- Admonish (warn, remind, or rebuke) the unruly
- Encourage the fainthearted
- Help the weak
- Don't repay evil for evil
- Seek what is good for one another and all people
- Have patience with everyone

- Rejoice always
- Never stop praying
- Give thanks in every circumstance
- Listen to the Holy Spirit
- Listen to prophecy, but fact check it seriously
- Cling to good
- Refrain from doing evil

If we try to make this a daily checklist, we will fail miserably. This is where that statement has a misunderstanding, however. Following Jesus because you love Him is entirely possible. Doing this allows you to read God's word in a new light.

When we recognize Jesus as the only answer to fulfillment, our own sin as the barrier that separates us from God, and our need for a perfect savior, it becomes easier to seek Jesus. The more time you spend in His word and His presence, the more you start falling in love with Jesus. He changes you, gives you new eyes to see the world, and convicts your heart in areas He knows you need to improve. Following after Him no longer becomes impossible. Yes, we have to die to sin daily and resist our flesh, but the more time we spend with Him, the easier it becomes.

All of these things Paul is referring to, is supposed to be a letter of encouragement to the church of Thessalonica. He wants them to aspire to these things together. This wasn't written to one person! We should be concerned about what the Bible says because we're called to be living it out in community with one another as a direct result of our love for Jesus. Jesus called you, and is faithful to bring you through it.

Spending time with Jesus and falling in love with the Bible are cute concepts, and ones our society generally accepts. The idea that following Jesus comes with a price, however, is where many people disengage. The truth is that Jesus didn't come to make your life sunshine and roses, He came to give you true life. You were a smelly dead corpse when Jesus met you. How He could love us in that state, I have no idea. He sacrificed everything for us, and we will find that following Him requires real sacrifice for us to.

Matthew 10:34-39

> *34 "Do not think that I came to bring peace on the earth; I did not come to bring peace, but a sword. 35 For I came to set a man against his father, and a daughter against her mother, and a daughter-in-law against her mother-in-law; 36 and a man's enemies will be the members of his household.*
> *37 "He who loves father or mother more than Me is not worthy of Me; and he who loves son or daughter more than Me is not worthy of Me. 38 And he who does not take his cross and follow after Me is not worthy of Me. 39 He who has found his life will lose it, and he who has lost his life for My sake will find it.*

In light of the freedom that He offers us from death, He never once said living would be easy. Choosing Jesus will sometimes be hard. Many of you will lose friends, family, and business relationships over this decision.

Sometimes people will break your front lawn ornaments because they want you to do something illegal instead of reporting them to the police.[35] Sometimes you will have to turn down business because of your convictions. Sometimes choosing Jesus means you'll be arrested, beaten, and potentially martyred.

The gravity of choosing Jesus is something we take all too lightly in America on a regular basis. Choosing Jesus isn't a life choice equivalent to becoming vegan. Choosing Jesus is something you should be able to stake your life and eternity on.

Living at peace with our Christian brothers and sisters (as Paul says) does not mean we will be naturally at peace with the world as well. Jesus is bringing a sword. So how do we

---

[35] A bit specific? This just happened to me while writing this chapter. At least I bought them on clearance!

prepare ourselves? Firstly, we must be rooted in the word of God regularly. When we are, it is easier to spot issues far on the horizon.

1 Corinthians 16:13-14

13 Be on the alert, stand firm in the faith, act like men, be strong. 14 Let all that you do be done in love.

We must act in love towards one another. Love, however, is not blind. We must be alert and strong. If we are going to be alert to potential threats, we need to prepare. We must surround ourselves with people who can encourage us to pursue the Lord and rebuke us when we are unruly. I cannot say how important it is for these people to be inside and outside your business.

2 Corinthians 6:14-16

14 Do not be bound together with unbelievers; for what partnership have righteousness and lawlessness, or what fellowship has light with darkness? 15 Or what harmony has Christ with Belial, or what has a believer in common with an unbeliever? 16 Or what agreement has the temple of God with idols? For we are the temple of the living God; just as God said, "I will dwell in them and walk among them; And I will be their God, and they shall be My people.

This doesn't mean that we should only work for and with Christians. Paul understands that this would be impossible (1 Corinthians 5:9-13). Letting people into your business with different values than yours, however, can cause major future issues. Being in any form of a binding contract with others will shape you. Choose those partnerships wisely, or it will cause unintentional animosity, frustration, and potentially legal implications.

Making decisions that honor the Lord will make people not like you. In business, there are certain people that we look to for their ironclad resolve, tenacity, steadfast endurance, resilience, steady hand, focus etc. These are respected character traits of a successful entrepreneur. Beating the odds is always the underdog story we cheer for. In the midst of it, no one actually ever wants to be the underdog though.

There is another side to this type of business owner, however, that can easily produce other names. Piledriver, dragon lady, bully, bossy, aggressive, mean, pushy, and stubborn are all a few that come to mind of those same people we can cheer so hard for as the underdog. Being resolved to follow Jesus, will mean you have to stand up for your biblical convictions. This doesn't mean you should be doing it in a disrespectful way, however.

The thing about business is that it usually equates to leadership in our society. The larger your business grows or reputation becomes, the bigger of a target you become. The media craves your carnage. We can easily look to the news to see how religious beliefs and affiliations can become the spotlight of a pathetically woven drama on a slow media day.

Being an open follower of Christ adds accountability to how you act and what you believe. Here's the thing though, if you're doing what's right, you have nothing to worry about (1 Peter 3:13-17). Jesus also says that the Holy Spirit will speak for us when this happens!

Matthew 10:16-20

16 "Behold, I send you out as sheep in the midst of wolves; so be shrewd as serpents and innocent as doves. 17 But beware of men, for they will hand you over to the courts and scourge you in their synagogues; 18 and you will even be brought before governors and kings for My sake, as a testimony to them and to the Gentiles. 19 But when they hand you over, do not worry about how or what you are to say; for it will be given you in that hour what you are to say. 20 For it is not you who speak, but it is the Spirit of your Father who speaks in you.

Today:

- Pray that God will work in your heart to see the Bible as an encouragement to your life in Christ.
- Praise Him for making us alive and for growing us.
- Praise God for the people in our lives that can give us accountability.
- Ask God to reveal to you the areas that your business needs to take a stand for righteousness.
- Pray for those who don't like you.
- Ask God to give you endurance in your walk with Him and the resolve to follow when times get tough.
- Praise God that we don't need to worry when other people speak negatively of us.
- Thank God that He will speak on our behalf when we are to testify for His sake.

DAY 17

The Doubt We Face

How many times have we seen something looming on the horizon and feared it's arrival or failure to arrive? Maybe it's a large accounts receivable that just won't pay you after all the work you did. Maybe it's hoping all the funds will be there to make payroll. Maybe it's a child getting sick while you're at a conference and your spouse asking you if taking off work is a good idea.

We start to wonder. Is this what I'm supposed to be doing? I am constantly feeling stressed. I have trouble falling asleep at night. Did God really call me to this? Will God really come through? Let's check out Psalm 77 to see what the Bible has to say about these types of feelings.

Psalm 77

> *1 My voice rises to God, and I will cry aloud; My voice rises to God, and He will hear me. 2 In the day of my trouble I sought the Lord; In the night my hand was stretched out without weariness; My soul refused to be comforted. 3 When I remember God, then I am disturbed; When I sigh, then my spirit*

grows faint. Selah.

4 You have held my eyelids open; I am so troubled that I cannot speak. 5 I have considered the days of old, The years of long ago. 6 I will remember my song in the night; I will meditate with my heart, And my spirit ponders: 7 Will the Lord reject forever? And will He never be favorable again? 8 Has His lovingkindness ceased forever? Has His promise come to an end forever? 9 Has God forgotten to be gracious, Or has He in anger withdrawn His compassion? Selah.

10 Then I said, "It is my grief, That the right hand of the Most High has changed." 11 I shall remember the deeds of the Lord; Surely I will remember Your wonders of old. 12 I will meditate on all Your work And muse on Your deeds. 13 Your way, O God, is holy; What god is great like our God? 14 You are the God who works wonders; You have made known Your strength among the peoples. 15 You have by Your power redeemed Your people, The sons of Jacob and Joseph. Selah.

16 The waters saw You, O God; The waters saw You, they were in anguish; The deeps also trembled. 17 The clouds poured out water; The skies gave forth a sound; Your arrows flashed here and there. 18 The sound of Your thunder was in the whirlwind; The lightnings lit up the world; The earth trembled and shook. 19 Your way was in the sea And Your paths in the mighty waters, And Your footprints may not be known. 20 You led Your people like a flock By the hand of Moses and Aaron.

This is my second or third time reading this Psalm all the way through, and I am seeing so many new things! We can tell that the writer is in serious despair. In fact, it sounds a lot like the things we were describing earlier. His eyelids are held open. He is so troubled he cannot speak. I actually love verse 3, "When I remember God, I moan; when I meditate, my spirit faints."

I have had those days where every time I think about the path God has placed before me, I don't really want to walk it. I feel overwhelmed, and a little disgruntled that He would make me do this. In these moments, I have been blessed to learn the following:

It's okay to have doubt. There is no shame in it, **but in order to find relief, you must keep seeking the Lord in your doubt, frustration, and despair**.

Verse 6 says, "let me meditate in my heart. Then my spirit made a diligent search." Diligence takes physical and emotional effort.

The writer asks himself questions about God. He wonders if God is even going to come through. These are questions based in doubt. Doubt is something everyone faces, and if handled properly, it can strengthen our faith for the next round of doubt we encounter. So how do we handle it?

We remember who God is. We recall the works of the past. We must remind ourselves of who God has been in the Bible and who His word says He is. His way is holy. He is the God who works wonders (verse 14). He is the redeemer of His people. The earth physically reacts at His presence. When He walks through the sea, His footprints are not seen! Even on our darkest days when we are angry about everything, we must remind ourselves who God is or we will not be able to fully overcome.

I remember one specific day when I had had it with everything God was doing in my business. I was done! I wrote EVERYTHING in my prayer journal. I ranted to God about how upset I was. You don't even know the level of upset I'm talking about right now. You're reading this and probably thinking, yeah, but this woman doesn't get upset like I do. Believe me, nobody had to teach me how to do this one!

After my rant, I literally had to force myself to ask these questions: What do I know is true? What does the Bible say is true? Who does God say He is? What does God say He will do?

This was forcing my brain into logic mode, outside of my emotions. It was painful. I think I cried harder here than I had through the rant, but it was worth it. I remembered who God was, and had the comfort to move forward, knowing He would give me the strength.

As you face insane frustration, and finish your rants, take time to ask yourself these questions:

- What do I know is true?
- What does the Bible say is true?
- Who does God say He is?
- What does God say He will do?

Today:
- Ask that God would work in your heart to seek Him while you are still frustrated.
- Pray that He would rid you of any self-righteous anger or justification for being upset with His plans.
- Praise God that it is not our responsibility to shoulder what He has called us to alone.
- Thank the Lord for being faithful to you even if you can't feel His presence or provision.
- Ask God to help you remember that He is still working when you feel discouraged.
- Pray that God would encourage you to press forward in His plan for your life and past your emotional state.

DAY 18

Abiding Daily

One summer, I worked full time as a program director of a summer camp. On some weekends, I would travel up to visit friends from my hometown. My grandparents happened to live (somewhat) on the way to the camp I was working at, and my mom always wanted me to stop by and visit them. There were two ways to get to my grandparents' house that ran parallel to one another.

One was the main road that everyone took. It had smoother, wider lanes, and trees trimmed farther back to help you watch out for deer that might be lurking in the woods. The other way was a bit like the backroads to nowhere, had more potholes, and limited cell phone reception. It also had beautiful trees close to the road, lakes, swamps, and animals. The key to the backroads, however, is that most tourists with their huge campers and boat trailers did not go this way. You would not get stuck behind a long line of traffic on a two-lane highway with oncoming traffic that never ended. For the full 2 ½ hours of driving, I always picked the back road.

On this particular sunny day, it was hot, but beautiful. As I drove, clouds started to roll out onto the sky. Soon it was sprinkling, then it was raining. By the time I got to the remote stretch of highway, the sky was greenish grey, the wind was rocking the trees farther than I had ever seen in my life, and the rain was hitting the ground so fast that you could not distinguish the edges of the road. I knew if the swamp overflowed, I would have little control over my vehicle, and could be pushed off the road into a river. I might not be able to get out or call for help.

My fingers were tight on the steering wheel, trying to distinguish where exactly the road was in front of me. I started praying. Almost directly in front of me, I faintly saw someone's red tail lights. I was not alone! Slowly the car inched forward, and I followed. The trees were violently whipping back and forth. We weaved past a few downed trees and kept pushing forward.

Suddenly, it dawned on me that this is how the earth responds to the presence of God. This was an incredible example of God's power and strength. *If God can do this, why am I freaking out? He knows exactly where I am, and He's in charge of all this!* My fear immediately subsided into amazed wonder. I still kept creeping forward, following the dim tail lights, but my entire perspective had shifted.

I was now watching the trees move in waves as the gusts of wind and rain pelted against them. Everything suddenly became magnificently orchestrated and beautiful to me. Here I was, privately witnessing the majesty of God's creation. I was positive that if He could display this much power through His creation, meeting Him today would be worth experiencing far more than anything this world had!

I was singing at the top of my lungs, praising the Lord, while I watched in amazement around me. The dim tail lights brought me into a small town where I waited inside a gas station for the rest of it to pass. There were probably 15 people waiting inside that gas station! All of us were amazed by the powerful storm.

Sometimes when things are uncomfortable or we are stretched too thin, our immediate response is to get tense and take control. We're determined to get through it, but when it's all on our shoulders, it gets pretty stressful.

This happens to me in business all the time. I try to take stock of what I have to get me through. Cell phone reception? Wiggle room in my annual budget? Educational material available? When I start looking into the situation, I realize my problem is actually my perspective. If I think I'm the one that needs to solve all these problems, I will continue to take on more responsibilities until I'm stressed and afraid. My business usually starts getting out of control when I lose my grasp on personal devotional time. My patience gets thinner, my time gets shorter, and my focus wanes.

John 15:1-11

> *1 "I am the true vine, and My Father is the vinedresser. 2 Every branch in Me that does not bear fruit, He takes away; and every branch that bears fruit, He prunes it so that it may bear more fruit. 3 You are already clean because of the word which I have spoken to you. 4 Abide in Me, and I in you. As the branch cannot bear fruit of itself unless it abides in the vine, so neither can you unless you abide in Me. 5 I am the vine, you are the branches; he who abides in Me and I in him, he bears much fruit, for apart from Me you can do nothing. 6 If anyone does not abide in Me, he is thrown away as a branch and dries up; and they gather them, and cast them into the fire and they are burned. 7 If you abide in Me, and My words abide in you, ask whatever you wish, and it will be done for you. 8 My Father is glorified by this, that you bear much fruit, and so prove to be My disciples. 9 Just as the Father has loved Me, I have also loved you; abide in My love. 10 If you keep My commandments, you will abide in My love; just as I have kept My Father's commandments and abide in His love. 11 These things I have spoken to you so that My joy may be in you, and that your joy may be made full.*

We cannot bear fruit if we choose to abide outside of Jesus. I want to define the word abide as John uses it. The Greek word for abide is ménō:

μένω **ménō,** men'-o; a primary verb; to stay (in a given place, state, relation or expectancy):—abide, continue, dwell, endure, be present, remain, stand, tarry (for)[36]

We must be present with Jesus in order to bear fruit. Why? Jesus says, "Apart from me you can do nothing." This means we need to spend time with Jesus. We do this by studying His word, praying, and seeking Him.

The two words that stick out to me as a business person are obedience and submission. Both are things I absolutely hate doing without trust. We cannot trust God, unless we get to know who He is. The world tells me that I am a strong, independent person. I can do anything I put my mind to. When I consider Paul's affliction, however, this is what he tells us God's response was:

2 Corinthians 12:9-10

> *9 And He has said to me, "My grace is sufficient for you, for power is perfected in weakness." Most gladly, therefore, I will rather boast about my weaknesses, so that the power of Christ may dwell in me. 10 Therefore I am well content with weaknesses, with insults, with distresses, with persecutions, with difficulties, for Christ's sake; for when I am weak, then I am strong*

The interesting thing about abiding in Christ, is that it's not just a simple do it, and be happy. While you are doing, you will be pruned! It sounds painful, but it is necessary to bear more fruit. Jesus essentially says, if you don't, you won't bear more fruit. A barren section of a vine needs to be cut out in order for the plant to remain healthy. What is the fruit? What does it look like? Well, we find similar verbiage in 1st John.

---

[36] Lexicon :: Strong's G3306 - menō. (2019). Retrieved from https://www.blueletterbible.org/lang/lexicon/lexicon.cfm?t=kjv&strongs=g3306

1 John 4:15-18

> *15 Whoever confesses that Jesus is the Son of God, God abides in him, and he in God. 16 We have come to know and have believed the love which God has for us. God is love, and the one who abides in love abides in God, and God abides in him. 17 By this, love is perfected with us, so that we may have confidence in the day of judgment; because as He is, so also are we in this world. 18 There is no fear in love; but perfect love casts out fear, because fear involves punishment, and the one who fears is not perfected in love.*

Here's the proof that we're taking the time to abide in God: Love. If we are abiding in God, His love will start pouring into our lives and out onto others. When we are abiding in God, His love is chasing away fear. Fears are usually accompanied by lies about what's going on around us. In business, it's really easy to slip into believing lies about other people's intentions, the tone of voice you received in an email, the motivation behind the person calling you, etc. My perception of the storm was completely altered when I knew who loved me and who was in control of it.

A few weeks after that incident, I chose to drive home on the main road. I was amazed. When that storm had gone through that area, all the beautifully trimmed trees had created a wind tunnel that caused them to splinter like toothpicks across the road. This was weeks later, and they were still cutting up and dragging away giant red pines! If I would have driven this road in the storm, I would have been crushed in a matter of minutes.

When I compare my circumstance to what God says about my place in His kingdom, I am blown away by how many lies slip away. God has a plan for your business, and is guiding you places that might seem terrifying, but are completely under His protection.

Today:

- Pray through this passage. Ask God to show you the lies you have been believing that have kept you from spending time in His presence.
- Ask forgiveness for the times you have tried to carry your business out of your own strength.
- Ask Him to help you abide in Him.

Isaiah 43:1-7

1 But now, thus says the Lord, your Creator, O Jacob, And He who formed you, O Israel, "Do not fear, for I have redeemed you; I have called you by name; you are Mine! 2 "When you pass through the waters, I will be with you; And through the rivers, they will not overflow you. When you walk through the fire, you will not be scorched, Nor will the flame burn you. 3 "For I am the Lord your God, The Holy One of Israel, your Savior; I have given Egypt as your ransom, Cush and Seba in your place. 4 "Since you are precious in My sight, Since you are honored and I love you, I will give other men in your place and other peoples in exchange for your life. 5 "Do not fear, for I am with you; I will bring your offspring from the east, And gather you from the west. 6 "I will say to the north, 'Give them up!' And to the south, 'Do not hold them back.' Bring My sons from afar And My daughters from the ends of the earth, 7 Everyone who is called by My name, And whom I have created for My glory, Whom I have formed, even whom I have made."

DAY 19

Productivity

A few years ago, I was able to sit in on a training with some exceptional sales people. The man next to me had won multiple awards for being a great salesperson and other business owners at the conference were consistently trying to poach him for their team. When I asked him why he liked his employer he told me, "He really cares about me. He's always looking out for my family, and our team is tight. Everyone encourages one another at my work. When I hit my goals this year, the owner bought me a truck! There's no way I would leave them."

Excellent people stay with your business because you acknowledge their excellence and treat them well. Excellent people continue to perform because they feel they are supported well to do so and incentivized properly.

At this point in the conference, I thought, "Well that's really cool, but there's no way everyone would be able be that kind of business owner." The next day, however, I was given the opportunity to hear this owner speak about how he runs his business. He started his business and it grew like crazy. They took on as many projects as they could, as fast as they could.

The trouble was, they had horrible follow through after a job was done. Quality was sacrificed in their rush, and their reviews tanked. They were making $12 million in gross, but netting less than $2 million. When an economic downturn hit, they were the last on the food chain to be given work. Their business took a nosedive.

The owner told us he was asked not to preach in this session, but through the language he used, I could tell this is the time where God had gotten ahold of his heart. After almost a complete company lay off, he revised his entire approach to business. They worked on creating processes, having solid training, and implementing accountability systems for every single employee to be recognized and reprimanded with.

He encouraged cost savings through incentivization, "If anyone has an idea to save the company money, I'm all ears. One day my team found a software that saved us over $1,000 a year. They asked if I would buy them lunch, and I said of course!"

He made a focused growth plan and strategically worked it out, ensuring they didn't make quality sacrifices as they increased in size.

He ended his presentation by saying. "Today, we have great customer reviews and quality work. It's taken us a few years, but today we're making a gross $12 million again and netting $7 million."

This is when I realized, everyone can be that kind of business owner! God had to tear down his business and rebuild it from the ground up in order for it to be successful. From speaking with his employees, I knew that complete God transformation is worth the effort. It takes complete surrender to the Lord in your business for Him to build it according to His plan. Dedication, structure, and self-control are all incredibly difficult things for visionary leaders, but God's planning and timing are way better than ours.

You could say his business was productive before, but when measured in sacrifice to his customers, employee's pride in their work, and overhead, this is a no brainer to which is better. Having a productive business starts with God transforming your heart, followed by Him transforming your organization. Jesus had some pretty clear things to say about how God manages people in the kingdom of heaven.

Matthew 25:14-30

14 "For it is just like a man about to go on a journey, who called his own slaves and entrusted his possessions to them. 15 To one he gave five talents, to another, two, and to another, one, each according to his own ability; and he went on his journey. 16 Immediately the one who had received the five talents went and traded with them, and gained five more talents. 17 In the same manner the one who had received the two talents gained two more. 18 But he who received the one talent went away, and dug a hole in the ground and hid his master's money.

19 "Now after a long time the master of those slaves came and settled accounts with them. 20 The one who had received the five talents came up and brought five more talents, saying, 'Master, you entrusted five talents to me. See, I have gained five more talents.' 21 His master said to him, 'Well done, good and faithful slave. You were faithful with a few things, I will put you in charge of many things; enter into the joy of your master.'

22 "Also the one who had received the two talents came up and said, 'Master, you entrusted two talents to me. See, I have gained two more talents.' 23 His master said to him, 'Well done, good and faithful slave. You were faithful with a few things, I will put you in charge of many things; enter into the joy of your master.'

24 "And the one also who had received the one talent came up and said, 'Master, I knew you to be a hard man, reaping where you did not sow and gathering where you scattered no seed. 25 And I was afraid, and went away and hid your talent in the ground. See, you have what is yours.'

26 "But his master answered and said to him, 'You wicked, lazy slave, you knew that I reap where I did not sow and gather where I scattered no seed. 27 Then you ought to have put my money in the bank, and on my arrival I would have received my money back with interest. 28 Therefore take away the talent from him, and give it to the one who has the ten talents.'

29 "For to everyone who has, more shall be given, and he will have an abundance; but from the one who does not have, even what he does have shall be taken away. 30 Throw out the worthless slave into the outer darkness; in that place there will be weeping and gnashing of teeth.

Here are the five takeaways that I think help give us a clear picture of how the master managed productivity:

1. The master gave responsibility to each according to their ability
2. Each was allowed to choose how to use their talent and was given time to see return on the investment
3. Those who successfully increased the master's investment were verbally recognized, and rewarded with further responsibility/promotion
4. The one who was afraid of taking risk and did nothing was removed
5. The one who was lazy, knew clearly the master's character and expectations

We see the master knew what each one was capable of handling. Can you imagine what a foolish decision it would have been to give the lazy servant the five talents and the exceptional servant one? It would have been a seriously missed ROI opportunity. The master also had patience with his servants by allowing them time to prove themselves. Return on investment takes time.

If the master would have said to the two successful slaves, "Thanks for your effort. I appreciate all the work you do," and moved on to the lazy slave, how do you think those who labored hard would have felt?

Acknowledgement should come with some sort of reward. Each person has different ways of feeling recognized; use all of them often. If hiring a new employee costs an average of $4,000 per worker[37], you can afford to acknowledge those who are productive and stay with your business.

If the master would have said to the lazy slave, "Oh, that's okay, we just need to work on your time management and give you more training."

How do you think it would have impacted the future performance of the other two servants? Refusing to keep people accountable for their actions when the expectations are clear will drop your entire business' productivity.

It affects morale and will leave the hard workers wondering why they are choosing to work so hard when other people don't. Your excellent workers will leave or worse, stay and lower their productivity to one step above lazy. Your unaccountable, unproductive workers set the productivity bar for everyone in your business.

The master is not a micromanager of his slaves, but here's the thing: **They all knew exactly what the master expected of them.**

If you're not setting the expectations and measurement systems in place, how will people know they have been successful with their talents? How will they be able to gauge their progress and feel they are doing well if you have not given them clear guidelines?

What's the best part for you? Clear accountability led to less work and stress for the master.

---

[37] How To Calculate Cost-Per-Hire (CPH). Glassdoor. (2018). Retrieved from https://www.glassdoor.com/employers/blog/calculate-cost-per-hire/

When the master returned, it was pretty clear who did their job well. The lazy slave had no room to say, "Well, you didn't tell me what you wanted." The master left no grey area. No excuse could cut it.

No HR party foul here! The master had provided clear expectations. He was able to unashamedly say, "You wicked, lazy slave, **you knew** that I reap where I did not sow and gather where I scattered no *seed.*"

There was justification to call him wicked and lazy. There was justification to let him go. Throwing the slave out into darkness where there is weeping and gnashing of teeth definitely sounds like an HR party foul in today's context. However, this parable is discussing how God handles people in His Kingdom. When we look at the other verses that discuss weeping and gnashing of teeth, we know that Jesus is referring to eternal separation from God in Hell.

In reviewing this passage for wisdom, we cannot forget this parable applies to us too. God has given you responsibilities according to your abilities, and what you do with it has eternal impacts. As a business owner you have been entrusted with much. Ensuring you are honoring the Lord with what has been entrusted to you has a greater impact than your bottom line.

When we look at the testimony of this man who turned his business around, it's not just about his numbers. It's about the incredible testimony of his employees.

People who say, "I would not leave this boss who cares about me."

I am willing to bet that when this sales person looks at the life of his boss, he knows exactly who his boss is following.[38] The Lord is magnified and glorified when people can look at

---

[38] When I see these kinds of moments in real life, it seriously just makes me want to do a fist pump and praise the Lord! Don't ever forget to tell others your business testimony. We need to be encouraged by what God is doing. What a beautiful thing to see Christ magnified!

you and point to Him.

Today:

- Praise God for giving you the responsibilities that you have.
- Ask God to give you the wisdom to grow your business strategically.
- Thank God that He can use the Bible to teach us about how He rewards and disciplines us!
- Praise God for your current employees and business partnerships that you work with regularly.
- Repent and ask God's forgiveness for the ways you have acted unjustly towards anyone.
- Ask God to train you in how to build your business according to His guidelines.
- Pray that God would show you how to recognize your employees and incentivize their efforts fairly.
- Ask God to show you the areas that your business requires attention in becoming accountable and increasing productivity.
- Pray that God would help you clearly reveal unproductive work within your business.
- Thank God for His provision, for His mercy, and for the clear expectations He has given us!

DAY 20

The Counterfeit Church

Last week, I sat down with some senior high school girls from my church and asked them this question: **What makes the church different from a humanitarian aid group, community center, or a business?**

After about an hour of discussion, Vietnamese food, and hot tea, they decided that the difference is the focus.[39] There are three parts to the church's focus. The number one goal of the church is to follow Christ. The number two goal is to tell other people about Christ. The third and final goal of the church is to encourage one another in our relationship with Christ. Everything else flows out of these crucial pieces.[40] When we start digging into the Bible, we

---

[39] Vietnamese food is usually a non-essential, but incredibly beneficial addition for any theological discussion.

[40] Can we just acknowledge that a group of high school students did this breakdown? I need to run more of my questions by them!

can see that this comes up everywhere!

John 20:31

> *31 but these have been written so that you may believe that Jesus is the Christ, the Son of God; and that believing you may have life in His name.*

1 John 5:13

> *13 These things I have written to you who believe in the name of the Son of God, so that you may know that you have eternal life.*

2 Corinthians 4:15

> *15 For all things are for your sakes, so that the grace which is spreading to more and more people may cause the giving of thanks to abound to the glory of God.*

Colossians 3:1-2 & 13-14

> *1 Therefore if you have been raised up with Christ, keep seeking the things above, where Christ is, seated at the right hand of God. 2 Set your mind on the things above, not on the things that are on earth...13 bearing with one another, and forgiving each other, whoever has a complaint against anyone; just as the Lord forgave you, so also should you. 14 Beyond all these things put on love, which is the perfect bond of unity.*

The church needs to focus on Jesus, tell others about him, and encourage one another's growth in Him. When the focus changes, it's bad.

James 4:1-5

> *1 What is the source of quarrels and conflicts among you? Is not the source your pleasures that wage war in your members? 2 You lust and do not have; so you commit murder. You are envious and cannot obtain; so you fight and quarrel. You do not have because you do not ask. 3 You ask and do not*

receive, because you ask with wrong motives, so that you may spend it on your pleasures. 4 You adulteresses, do you not know that friendship with the world is hostility toward God? Therefore whoever wishes to be a friend of the world makes himself an enemy of God. 5 Or do you think that the Scripture speaks to no purpose: "He jealously desires the Spirit which He has made to dwell in us"?

Philippians 2:4 & 12

4 do not merely look out for your own personal interests, but also for the interests of others...12 So then, my beloved, just as you have always obeyed, not as in my presence only, but now much more in my absence, work out your salvation with fear and trembling;

Hebrews 10:23-24

23 Let us hold fast the confession of our hope without wavering, for He who promised is faithful; 24 and let us consider how to stimulate one another to love and good deeds, 25 not forsaking our own assembling together, as is the habit of some, but encouraging one another; and all the more as you see the day drawing near.

Not only do we have to encourage one another, Hebrews says we should not forsake assembling together in order to do just that! Here's the thing that I foresee happening to some of you, however. Some of you are thinking, *I have the body of Christ around me every day. My business is my ministry."*

Yes, every part of our life should be a sacrifice to God (Romans 12:1-2), but what most of you mean by this statement is far deeper. In your heart, you mean, "My business is my church. I don't have to go anywhere else or give any of my time anywhere else."

I will fight you on this, every time. **If anything besides** those 3 priorities of the church are a part of your organization, you're either doing church wrong or you are pretending it's a church. The bride of Christ is something special.

2 Corinthians 11:2

> *2 For I am jealous for you with a godly jealousy; for I betrothed you to one husband, so that to Christ I might present you as a pure virgin.*

Ephesians 5:25-27

> *25 Husbands, love your wives, just as Christ also loved the church and gave Himself up for her, 26 so that He might sanctify her, having cleansed her by the washing of water with the word, 27 that He might present to Himself the church in all her glory, having no spot or wrinkle or any such thing; but that she would be holy and blameless.*

Here's the thing, if every document has to have your signature on it for approval, odds are, this is not Christ's bride.[41] Let's define Christ's bride: The body of Christ.

Ephesians 1:22-23

> *22 And He put all things in subjection under His feet, and gave Him as head over all things to the church, 23 which is His body, the fullness of Him who fills all in all.*

Jesus is the head of the body. The body of Christ is also called the church.

1 Corinthians 12:12-14

> *12 For even as the body is one and yet has many members, and all the*

---

[41] If the odds are in your favor, you're probably leading a cult. You need more Bible teaching than the 1,000 scripture verses or less (granted through copy write laws of the NASB translation) to tackle this kind of issue.

members of the body, though they are many, are one body, so also is Christ.
13 For by one Spirit we were all baptized into one body, whether Jews or
Greeks, whether slaves or free, and we were all made to drink of one Spirit.
14 For the body is not one member, but many.
The body of Christ has many members and one Holy Spirit. We are part of the
body through Christ.

Colossians 3:15-16

15 Let the peace of Christ rule in your hearts, to which indeed you were
called in one body; and be thankful. 16 Let the word of Christ richly dwell
within you, with all wisdom teaching and admonishing one another with
psalms and hymns and spiritual songs, singing with thankfulness in your
hearts to God.

1 Corinthians 6:15

15 Do you not know that your bodies are members of Christ? Shall I then take
away the members of Christ and make them members of a prostitute? May it
never be!

If these 3 points are what distinguish the church, and the focus is solely Jesus Christ, nothing else could ever be the church, including your business. You need to be in community with the body of Christ. People have accountability to Christ and to one another in the church.

Entrepreneurs regularly share new ideas and come into conflict with others. It can be healthy conflict, but it still happens. People regularly become entrepreneurs because they hate authority, "I want to be my own boss!" Peter happens to write about people who don't like authority, and it just so happens that Jesus actually said Peter would be the rock on which he would build the church (Matt. 16:18).

2 Peter 2:9

9 then the Lord knows how to rescue the godly from temptation, and to keep

*the unrighteous under punishment for the day of judgment, 10 and especially
those who indulge the flesh in its corrupt desires and despise authority.*

The Lord knows how to keep those who despise authority under punishment for the day of
judgment! Reality check, as a business owner, you will come into contact with people your
personality clashes against. Reality check, as a Christ follower, you are called to fellowship
with a body of believers, even if they have a different perspective than you. Your role in the
church has submission to Christ written all over it. Get over yourself and contribute to the
body!

1 Corinthians 12:4-7

*4 Now there are varieties of gifts, but the same Spirit. 5 And there are
varieties of ministries, and the same Lord. 6 There are varieties of effects, but
the same God who works all things in all persons. 7 But to each one is given
the manifestation of the Spirit for the common good.*

Did you see that? There are a variety of gifts, ministries, and effects (ways to go about it)!
All come from the same God for the common good. Yes! We're on the same team![42]

Your spiritual gifts are a manifestation of the Holy Spirit in you, to be used for His glory in
brotherly love. If you choose not to contribute to the body of Christ and only to your
business, you are short-sighted and have forgotten that you were cleansed from your sins (2
Peter 1:2-9). If you actually see other people's spiritual gifts play out, all are jaw dropping.

Here's the truth: You won't have many opportunities to see people's spiritual gifts play out

---

[42] This is so good! When I read this, it made me start fist pumping. I even did some ballet
spins, and rejoicing! Then, I got dizzy because I can't focus on one object whilst spinning.
Pretty sure that pho I just ate is having some words with my tummy now. Praise God
anyways!

if you aren't in fellowship with the church! Yes, sometimes you will see glimpses of them in business, but their purpose is to edify the church (1 Cor. 14:12).

The other day, I was reading a book where the writer said she and her husband felt called to set a goal to live off 50% of their income and give the rest away. This is the spiritual gift of giving! Jaw dropping to everyone else. Amazing, and for most of us, unfathomable.

My husband has the spiritual gift of faith. He never worries about the future. He never second guesses God's goodness and love for him. He never has doubts about the Bible's accuracy and authenticity. He does not worry about God's provision. He sees me freaking out all the time, is concerned for my well-being, but never waivers in his resolve to trust that God knows what He's doing. To live 100%, worry free about the future blows my mind.

My father-in-law has the gift of evangelism. He can talk to a random stranger and within 5 minutes that person can start weeping and relaying his or her entire life story. He casually brings the gospel into conversation and people are shocked at the clarity it brings to their thoughts. His stories are amazing.

The body of Christ's spiritual gifts should be inspiring to us and motivating us to seek the Lord further. This is beautiful. We are also not expected to have every spiritual gift! We won't be able to do everything, and that's because each is only one piece of the body (1 Corinthians 12:14-22). Every hand needs a foot, or it will only reach for things it cannot move to attain.

Knowing your personality strengths and weaknesses can also help you understand how to use your spiritual gifts in a more productive way in the church and understand why you clash with certain people. Personality tests are so beneficial to understanding how your brain works, what bothers you, who you need to support you, and what your "go to mode" in times of stress looks like.

The more you know about who God made you to be, the easier it is to have grace for other people and recognize the reasons behind your emotions. Just remember your personality is the explanation, NOT THE EXCUSE. Choosing to act like a weenie to other people because, "that's just the way God made me" is complete rubbish.[43] We must understand that God has gifted all for His glory before we can fully appreciate how other people's gifts can glorify God and move the body forward under the leadership of Christ.

Today:

- Ask God how He wants you to be contributing to your local church.
- Thank God that He has given you gifts to use.
- Praise Him for making the body of Christ completely focused on Christ.
- Thank Him that He is the head of the church.
- Pray that He would use your personality and spiritual gifts to be an encouragement to others as they pursue Christ.
- Ask God to strip your heart of any pride you have in your abilities and knowledge.
- Pray that He would teach you to be humble before Him and before those in church leadership over you.

---

[43] My husband said it was okay to say weenie. If you have a beef with it, please rest assured, this one is only mechanically separated pork. #pun

DAY 21

The Accountability of Branding

People who claim to be Christians and act contrary to what the Bible describes are a definite problem many of us have experienced. It makes me cringe even more when people start doing this in business. To this day, when people tell me that they are a Christian in business, my first initial instinct is to trust them less. Where business and religious faith connect has so many layers. To slap the label "Christian" onto your business is to invite criticism and accountability when you're doing it wrong.

Here are two common ways people misuse the brand of Christianity:

A.   Using it as an excuse to make people act or do certain things for you

B.   Using it to gain something without actually living out a Christ like life

Jesus didn't use who he was as the reason for people to change their lives. If you look through the gospels, you will find that spending time with Jesus was what made people decide they wanted to make life changes, not His constant name dropping that He was the son of God. You will find the perfect example of this in the man Zacchaeus.

Luke 19:1-10

> *1 He entered Jericho and was passing through. 2 And there was a man called by the name of Zaccheus; he was a chief tax collector and he was rich. 3 Zaccheus was trying to see who Jesus was, and was unable because of the crowd, for he was small in stature. 4 So he ran on ahead and climbed up into a sycamore tree in order to see Him, for He was about to pass through that way. 5 When Jesus came to the place, He looked up and said to him, "Zaccheus, hurry and come down, for today I must stay at your house." 6 And he hurried and came down and received Him gladly. 7 When they saw it, they all began to grumble, saying, "He has gone to be the guest of a man who is a sinner." 8 Zaccheus stopped and said to the Lord, "Behold, Lord, half of my possessions I will give to the poor, and if I have defrauded anyone of anything, I will give back four times as much." 9 And Jesus said to him, "Today salvation has come to this house, because he, too, is a son of Abraham. 10 For the Son of Man has come to seek and to save that which was lost."*

Zaccheus was Jewish. To be Jewish and to decide to work for the Roman government (who was, at the time, responsible for repression of Israel) was to basically be the founder of the American Lung Association's child and be advertising for Marlboro. It was a move that would hurt your political relationships and potentially close family associations.

Zaccheus could do decent accounting work, which means he was smart. He was in charge of people as the head tax collector, which means the Roman government trusted him enough for the job to make him a manager. The guy wasn't a bum living under a bridge, he was a dirty CFO who happened to be very financially successful. People knew he was crooked. His employees were overtaxing and taking a cut for themselves and for him!

In a day with no social media or news casting, it was sometimes easy to get around unnoticed as a crooked business person. It had to go by word of mouth and association with your name. Even then, there might be more than one Zaccheus! He had an additional problem, though. He was small in stature. If you didn't know it was him, it wouldn't take much effort to think through the list of known people identified as being short. It's no wonder people were crowding him out from being able to see Jesus. He has to climb a tree in order to see anything.

Jesus sees him and says, "Come down because I'm staying at your house today." Can you imagine the outrage? People are upset. That'd be like Jesus saying to a government approved Bernie Madoff, "Let's have brunch." When Zaccheus spent time with Jesus, however, he had a change of heart!

Think of what a testimony it would be for a guy who was legally untouchable to decide to pay everyone back four times the amount that he had cheated them out of. Talk about a great interest rate! He saw what Jesus had to offer and decided to change. There is no mention that Jesus had a chat with him about his life. Something in Zaccheus changed after simply being around Jesus! Jesus closes their time together by saying, "Today salvation has come to this house, since he also is a son of Abraham. For the Son of Man came to seek and to save the lost."

Jesus didn't come to put people on a guilt trip. He came to save them.

1 John 4:7-9

> *7 Beloved, let us love one another, for love is from God; and everyone who loves is born of God and knows God. 8 The one who does not love does not know God, for God is love. 9 By this the love of God was manifested in us, that God has sent His only begotten Son into the world so that we might live through Him.*

Our job as Christ followers is to testify of Jesus. We do this in love. He is the manifestation of love. Therefore, we are like Him and testify of Him when we live in love. If we can get "love" figured out, our actions should speak volumes about who we follow. Jesus says that in verse 35 of John 13!

John 13:34-35

> *34 A new commandment I give to you, that you love one another, even as I have loved you, that you also love one another. 35 By this all men will know that you are My disciples, if you have love for one another."*

Who runs the conviction department of your business? The answer to this question is and always should be the HOLY SPIRIT. Not you, not your managers or your leadership team, and certainly not your employee handbook. Does that mean we never openly talk about Jesus and just let our actions do the talking? No, but if we are talking about Jesus, it should include our relationship with Him and how He is changing us. You should not be using your words to attempt conviction in someone else's heart. This is passive aggressive, and it's not your job.

Love does not mean we fail to have accountability within our businesses. No, loving people means that we must be just and fair in our business practices and policies. You cannot love well without having accountability, discipline, and rewards.

Hebrews 12:6-11

> *6 For those whom the Lord loves He disciplines, And He scourges every son whom He receives." 7 It is for discipline that you endure; God deals with you as with sons; for what son is there whom his father does not discipline? 8 But if you are without discipline, of which all have become partakers, then you are illegitimate children and not sons. 9 Furthermore, we had earthly fathers to discipline us, and we respected them; shall we not much rather be subject to the Father of spirits, and live? 10 For they disciplined us for a short time as seemed best to them, but He disciplines us for our good, so that we may share His holiness. 11 All discipline for the moment seems not to be joyful, but sorrowful; yet to those who have been trained by it, afterwards it yields the peaceful fruit of righteousness.*

Hebrews 12 says that God disciplines those He loves. Sometimes love is painful, but it will yield a fruit of righteousness. To love, is to have healthy conflict.

Sometimes businesses try to use the name Christianity to gain something from others. If you are a God-fearing and openly professing Christ follower, you better believe HR should be the first place you are honoring others. In discipline and in reward, you must always hold to your business standards and core values. If there is an excuse that you cannot fight, you have not built a strong enough accountability system within your business. If the contract says it, or if the law states it, you better be doing it.

If you own a business, you are in a position of leadership that makes serious decisions about the future of your employees. If you place a non-follower of Christ (or one who is for that matter) in submission to a proclaiming Christian, you better hope that leader is pointing to Christ the way the Bible says to.

If people look at you and think they see Christ's work, you better pray they are right. When Christian business owners fail to uphold an agreement or a legally binding contract, it is an intentional confusion to who a Christian should be and a poor reflection of the gospel. Treating people poorly while claiming the name of Christ distorts the message of the gospel and can turn people away from an eternal decision. Leaders have a stricter judgement before God in their actions (James 3:1-2). Your attention to this aspect of your life and business is a serious matter.

If lawsuits come at you solely because you're a Christian business owner, you should not have anything to fear in the United States. Are you being persecuted for your faith? Maybe. Often times, however, people do things in the name of Christ without being obedient to the processes that the government has set in place to handle them correctly.

Romans 13:1-5

1 Every person is to be in subjection to the governing authorities. For there is no authority except from God, and those which exist are established by God. 2 Therefore whoever resists authority has opposed the ordinance of God; and they who have opposed will receive condemnation upon themselves. 3 For rulers are not a cause of fear for good behavior, but for evil. Do you want to have no fear of authority? Do what is good and you will have praise from the same; 4 for it is a minister of God to you for good. But if you do what is evil, be afraid; for it does not bear the sword for nothing; for it is a minister of God, an avenger who brings wrath on the one who practices evil. 5 Therefore it is necessary to be in subjection, not only because of wrath, but also for conscience' sake.

Going against the government is going against a God appointed authority. As I have read many accounts of business owners outside the United States who truly do face some serious problems with government rules and regulations, I am firstly reminded how blessed we are in the U.S. Secondly, I am reminded that prayer and wisdom are the things necessary for facing animosity towards your business or your faith. Commonly these difficult issues come from misunderstandings, misinformation, or previous negative experiences. Having grace and respect for those in authority allows you to listen and understand their perspective. When people feel heard and respected, they become a lot less scary to be around!

The reality is, if we choose to place a representation label on our business or ourselves, we need to evaluate how we are representing that brand often.

Today:
- Ask God to show you how to represent Christ in your business accurately.
- Ask God to reveal to you the areas where you have not made your business accountable to upholding righteous business practices.
- Pray that God would show you where you are representing the gospel poorly.
- Ask that He would help you to love others and point to Him through your actions.
- Ask that He would help you keep your actions accountable in ensuring your business treats employees and customers justly.
- Thank God that He has placed government authority over us to guide us in treating others fairly.

DAY 22

Safeguards

The bigger they are the harder they fall. This saying could not be truer in business. Why? Because the ethical responsibility to customers, employees, and partners is important in our society. When I was in college, I studied abroad in Ireland. In one class on change management, I learned how immensely different the United States is from Europe in regards to morality.

Together, we dissected how Europe was shocked at the way the United States media shredded President Bill Clinton over his actions with Monica Lewinsky. Europeans couldn't understand why the United States was making such a big deal about this. The final proposed reason behind this perspective was, "It's not shocking because everybody does it. That shouldn't affect his ability to do a good job in politics. Personal and professional things should be separate."

As a culture, there are times where God's ethical standard is actually matched by society. Don't steal, don't lie, and don't kill people. Most cultures seem to agree on these concepts. Your moral responsibility before God, however, is a big deal. God cares deeply about the decisions you make. Regardless of if they are popular in society or not, our moral compass needs to be directed by the word of God. Without it, we are left to the mercy of society's flippant opinions and values that change based on the individual that is speaking. **If truth is relative to the one speaking, it is not the truth.**

In John 17, we find Jesus talking to God. He's praying for his disciples.

John 17:14-19

> *14 I have given them Your word; and the world has hated them, because they are not of the world, even as I am not of the world. 15 I do not ask You to take them out of the world, but to keep them from the evil one. 16 They are not of the world, even as I am not of the world. 17 Sanctify them in the truth; Your word is truth. 18 As You sent Me into the world, I also have sent them into the world. 19 For their sakes I sanctify Myself, that they themselves also may be sanctified in truth.*

Okay, now, firstly you have to believe that God's word is inerrant and God-breathed. If you believe the Bible is from God, then you need to believe that it is the ultimate source of truth. In this passage, we find Jesus is praying that his disciples would be sanctified in it. In case you didn't know, sanctification is the act or process of becoming holy. I'm breaking out into major excitement over here! If we want to be holy, we need to be in the truth, which is the word of God. For all the visual learners and mathematicians:

God's Word = Truth + Sanctification = HOLINESS

In the business world, there are many people that can help you identify ways to improve your business. I remember one of my first encounters with a business coach. He told us that he once worked with a business that needed to change its culture. The business owner's employees were stealing, not working hard, had a negative attitude, and were self-entitled in every concept of the word. The coach worked and worked with this team to try to cultivate a positive culture to no avail. After months of strategy and reviewing the business' financial documents, the business coach was discouraged.

He told the owner that he wasn't sure where the issue was coming from, but it was the source of everyone's behavior. If it did not surface soon, the business would need to lay off employees. The owner started to weep. As he did, he told the business coach that for some time, he had been cheating on his wife with his secretary. His staff knew about it. They had lost their respect for him and as a result, lost their desire to see the business succeed.

John 3:19-21

> *19 This is the judgment, that the Light has come into the world, and men loved the darkness rather than the Light, for their deeds were evil. 20 For everyone who does evil hates the Light, and does not come to the Light for fear that his deeds will be exposed. 21 But he who practices the truth comes to the Light, so that his deeds may be manifested as having been wrought in God."*

If we practice truth, we will not be ashamed of the light. Who is the light? If we back up a few chapters in John, we find that it is Jesus.

John 1:1-5

> *1 In the beginning was the Word, and the Word was with God, and the Word was God. 2 He was in the beginning with God. 3 All things came into being through Him, and apart from Him nothing came into being that has come into being. 4 In Him was life, and the life was the Light of men. 5 The Light shines in the darkness, and the darkness did not comprehend it.*

There will be times that the world will not understand the things you do to be in the light as a business. Last year, I drove 4 hours out of the way to pick up my mom for a conference I was attending. This year, I paid for an extra plane ticket to take my mom with me to a conference. It did not make financial sense. Why pay more for someone to come with? In my specific situation, I will tell you that these conferences had a target market of primarily men. There are many people that attend and leave their wedding rings at home.

It is unfortunate, but actually not uncommon in many industries. I need safeguards in my life that the world will not always understand. Also, I have found a great test of someone's intentions when they are interested in talking business with you is to tell them you're traveling with your mom. It actually increases my productivity in weeding out those who could waste my time! There's a cost savings right there!

Paul adds to this idea in Ephesians. (Clarification: He adds to the idea of the world and the light, not traveling with your mom.)

Ephesians 4:17-18

17 So this I say, and affirm together with the Lord, that you walk no longer just as the Gentiles also walk, in the futility of their mind, 18 being darkened in their understanding, excluded from the life of God because of the ignorance that is in them, because of the hardness of their heart;

Boom. The ignorance that is in them darkens their understanding of your actions. So, what do we need to do? Well, Paul helps us figure that out as we keep reading. I'm going to focus on the specifics of our current topic, but I really would love for you to read the entire chapter on your own because there's just so much more there!

Ephesians 4:25-27

25 Therefore, laying aside falsehood, speak truth each one of you with his neighbor, for we are members of one another. 26 Be angry, and yet do not sin; do not let the sun go down on your anger, 27 and do not give the devil an opportunity.

Wow! What a guy! He seems to be telling us exactly the same thing that John was! We should be not only living truth, we should be speaking it! On top of that, he's got some great further direction. We should give no opportunity to the devil! If there is a place in your business that you know you could fall short, you need to address it.

Remember the SWOT analysis? You should be looking into that on a personal level. Just as these weaknesses will change with the size of your business, so will your personal ones. Where are YOUR weaknesses? How can you safeguard yourself?

Today:

- You need to draw out your SWOT analysis in the weakness category and review it with your spouse (if you have one), accountability partners, and those you work with the closest.
- Ask God to give them wisdom in helping you safeguard your future as a business owner and a follower of Jesus.
- Praise God that He has given you people to remind you of your commitment to Christ!
- Thank God for protecting you from yourself and the pain that you can bring to your own life.
- Praise the Lord for providing the Holy Spirit and not leaving us without a Helper.

DAY 23

Work Life Balance

My parents are quite the pair. My dad was a pre-med student who T.A.'ed my mom's nursing class and ended up convincing her to marry him. About 5 kids into their marriage, my dad got a job in a new strange land.[44] Upon moving across the country, buying a house, and working for 6 months, the company announced to the clinic staff that the entire company was filing for bankruptcy due to embezzlement. Everyone's jobs ended that day. We had one house still for sale and had just moved into the new one!

My parents frantically planned how to keep us afloat, and finally decided to start their own business by opening a clinic. Healthcare for rural America! If you have ever been on a medical mission trip to a different country, I would say this encapsulates my childhood well.

---

[44] Sometimes it's easier for me to denote time by the number of siblings that were present. There are 7 of us, so each child seemed to denote a new stage in our lifetime. Some of you will understand.

People found random medical equipment in their basements and would drop it off for us to use. We even re-did the clinic floors in free turquoise and bright purple tile!

What my parents did not know, is that insurance companies are notorious for paying 6 months after being invoiced. With little to nothing left, our first house finally sold, and we were miraculously able to survive the wait.

As business started to pick up, we had to hire a receptionist. Praise God for that woman. She was excellent at corralling phones and 5 children when she had to. I distinctly remember a time when I had written all my spelling words out on a notebook and pressed down as hard as I could. If I angled it just right, I could see the impression of the words on the next blank page as I took my test.

In an attempt to sneak past my mom's uncanny eye, I tried to take my spelling test with the receptionist. No wool was pulled over her eyes! I was reported abruptly, and spanked by my mother accordingly. To this day, when I see naughty children of business owners, I have a hard time holding my tounge.

Work and life meet in a very interesting way for a business owner. It is different than the average person to be sure. There are times that your personal will spill over into your professional day more than others, but are there any guidelines in the Bible that help us figure this out?

Well, it just so happens, as I was reading Proverbs one day, I found a pretty decent description of an entrepreneur with wise life balance! The passage felt like it was jumping off the page at me the first time I read it through the lens of entrepreneurship.

Proverbs 31:10-31

> *10 An excellent wife, who can find? For her worth is far above jewels. 11 The heart of her husband trusts in her, And he will have no lack of gain. 12 She does him good and not evil All the days of her life. 13 She looks for wool and flax And works with her hands in delight. 14 She is like merchant ships; She brings her food from afar. 15 She rises also while it is still night And gives*

food to her household And portions to her maidens. 16 She considers a field and buys it; From her earnings she plants a vineyard. 17 She girds herself with strength And makes her arms strong. 18 She senses that her gain is good; Her lamp does not go out at night. 19 She stretches out her hands to the distaff, And her hands grasp the spindle. 20 She extends her hand to the poor, And she stretches out her hands to the needy. 21 She is not afraid of the snow for her household, For all her household are clothed with scarlet. 22 She makes coverings for herself; Her clothing is fine linen and purple. 23 Her husband is known in the gates, When he sits among the elders of the land. 24 She makes linen garments and sells them, And supplies belts to the tradesmen. 25 Strength and dignity are her clothing, And she smiles at the future. 26 She opens her mouth in wisdom, And the teaching of kindness is on her tongue. 27 She looks well to the ways of her household, And does not eat the bread of idleness. 28 Her children rise up and bless her; Her husband also, and he praises her, saying: 29 "Many daughters have done nobly, But you excel them all." 30 Charm is deceitful and beauty is vain, But a woman who fears the Lord, she shall be praised. 31 Give her the product of her hands, And let her works praise her in the gates.

This specific chapter of the Bible describes what it can tangibly look like to be a good wife. The concepts that are provided give us a clear picture of different attributes the Bible recognizes to be a good thing! Guess what?! Working can be a good thing! We don't need to guilt ourselves out of enjoying it.

I would like you to read the phrase "work life balance can mean" before reading each of these bullet points:

- Having a good relationship with your spouse and seeking to do good to him or her.
- Having joy in working.
- Providing for your family and staff even if it means having to get up earlier and staying up later.

- Understanding how to make good investments, see return, and invest again.
- Your work should build your strength and give you discernment on what decisions were a good idea.
- Helping the poor and needy.
- Planning for the future and making sure your family is ready for what's next.
- You should be an upright person in your community and help your spouse feel respected in the community as well.
- Strength and dignity should power your business.
- Looking at the future should be something to look forward to.
- Only allowing what is good, such as wisdom and kindness, to come from your mouth.
- Looking out for your family's and employee's needs and anticipating them.
- You are working hard.
- Your children and your spouse praise the work you are doing.
- You fear the Lord.
- The quality of your products speaks of your great reputation.

This passage discusses a wife that also is an entrepreneur. Her business is intertwined into one full life. There is no such thing as a personal and a professional life. They are one in the same. She is dignified in any sphere she enters. Her joy comes because of previous preparation and strategy. Her family respects her in what she is doing because she openly seeks to meet their needs. They are all actively taking part in her entrepreneurship in some way.

This business woman is diversified in more ways than one! She is productive in the morning and at night. She does what it takes to ensure her staff and family are ready for the future. Your family is not meant to be separated from your business, but they also have roles to play in your home and in the community.

It is your role to encourage others in their understanding of the incredible love of Christ and actively let this love play out in your life. There is no greater role than this. It will happen inside and outside your business. To leave this to someone else is to shirk your responsibility. There are many wonderful people who can support you in this journey, but they are not directing the path you will take.

Some of you have glossed over this chapter because you are single or don't have children. If you're single, praise God! It means your thoughts can be more on the works of God (1 Corinthians 7:32-35). The fact is, singleness, marriage, children, your church, or your business, is not the fulfillment of the Christian life; Jesus is.

You are not without family, however. Your local church is the body of Christ that needs you and you need them. I don't have any biological children yet, but God has called us to minister to so many children for this season of our lives. God will place younger people in your life that need your wisdom and instruction. If you will not guide them, the world is certainly willing to!

Work life balance shouldn't be about the amount of time spent with family versus spent on business. Work life balance will look different for every single person. Every family has different needs and every business has specific requirements.

Psalm 127:1-2

> *1 Unless the Lord builds the house, They labor in vain who build it; Unless the Lord guards the city, The watchman keeps awake in vain. 2 It is vain for you to rise up early, To retire late, To eat the bread of painful labors; For He gives to His beloved even in his sleep.*

If you choose to put God first, He will guide you through the balance of what your family and business need from you. He will teach you to anticipate their needs and move forward in His timing, but if you aren't putting God first, you are working in vain.

Today:

- Pray about how God wants you to actively take part in sharing the love of Christ with your family.
- Ask God to show you how you can serve your family and prepare for the future.
- Thank God that He will teach us when we seek Him.
- Pray for those who have helped to teach you and for those God has called you to teach.
- Pray that God would help you to identify your household's needs as they arise. Thank God for His provision.
- Praise Him for His faithfulness and for allowing your family and business to glorify His name.
- Pray for those within your business that you are mentoring, and other children in your life God can use you to impact.
- Pray that they would see the love of Christ acted out in your life.

DAY 24

When You Lose It

Much to my chagrin, I am the queen of losing it. When I am neck deep in stressful situations, it's not long before I have the urge to do something drastic. This happens a lot when I feel there is too much clutter in my house. I start feeling overwhelmed as I trip on things, and put stuff away, until I finally cannot handle it anymore. I just start throwing things in the garbage as fast as I find them. I think about getting rid of the dog because there is too much work in cleaning up dog hair. I go through the cupboards and pitch whatever looks like it's old, and root through the basement to see what collection of things I can give the boot. Everyone treads lightly when I get into frantic mode, because there is a high probability that they will get put to work as well.

Losing it comes in many forms. I used to be someone that lost it in just about any situation. Every time I start to feel like I'm getting a handle on losing it, something else happens. God is very good at pointing out the areas in our life where we still need to work on frustration, anger, unforgiveness, and lack of patience. For some of us, this can lead to a continual dread of losing it. We worry that we are one step away from losing our cool.

Today, I'm not going to tell you that you should never listen to this concern. I believe it is important to test this concern regularly. If you find yourself being convicted about the potential to say something hurtful, this could be meant as a warning before it's too late.

We are told not to live in worry or fear (Matt. 6:25-36). We don't need to live in constant fear about our inability to keep it together. If you've "lost it" in the past, it can be easy to slip into "low risk mode." This is where you choose to avoid anything and everything that may trigger you. This is not how God intends for us to live. It is also the place where business owners can plateau. We don't like to admit when we were wrong or apologize, so we avoid taking risks or interacting with other people. Did you know God can still use these broken moments to glorify His name when we choose to apologize?

Thinking back on my life, I know this to be true. I have inherited my dad's temper. My dad is a 6'2," football build, bearded man. He has a booming voice that can be heard on the line of scrimmage during a college football game. When my dad is even a little grouchy, he looks grouchy. I have seen my dad lose it.

I distinctly remember a time we went to a wrestling meet and he challenged the ref about a call that he considered bias. He actually was so loud in arguing that he was asked to leave the gym. I remember driving home with him after the meet in silence.

We drove to the school, and he got out to speak to the coach. He apologized for his actions and asked for forgiveness. The interesting thing was, the coach responded by saying, "It takes a man of character to actually admit when he is wrong. I have more respect for you than I have for most parents. I appreciate the apology. We all get out of hand sometimes."

End of story? No. My dad missed the assistant coach, so we drove to his house! He knocked on his front door to ask for forgiveness. He even asked my brother for forgiveness for acting that way at his wrestling meet when we got home.

My dad has lost it quite a few times throughout my life, but he's never failed to recognize it and apologize. I praise God for that. Even though it's not God's desire for him to lose it, he has consistently brought attention to how God can intervene in his heart and humble him to seek forgiveness. It has taught me a lot about how to respond after I have messed up.

James 1:19-26

> *19 This you know, my beloved brethren. But everyone must be quick to hear, slow to speak and slow to anger; 20 for the anger of man does not achieve the righteousness of God. 21 Therefore, putting aside all filthiness and all that remains of wickedness, in humility receive the word implanted, which is able to save your souls. 22 But prove yourselves doers of the word, and not merely hearers who delude themselves. 23 For if anyone is a hearer of the word and not a doer, he is like a man who looks at his natural face in a mirror; 24 for once he has looked at himself and gone away, he has immediately forgotten what kind of person he was. 25 But one who looks intently at the perfect law, the law of liberty, and abides by it, not having become a forgetful hearer but an effectual doer, this man will be blessed in what he does.*

> *26 If anyone thinks himself to be religious, and yet does not bridle his tongue but deceives his own heart, this man's religion is worthless.*

We find the Bible says that the anger of man does not produce God's righteousness. How do we deal with this issue of anger? James tells us right there! We need to be receiving the word of God and actually DOING IT! In order to get better and improve over time, we need to be reading and practicing the word, not just agreeing with it as a good concept!

The passage keeps going to talk in verse 26 about how we also need to bridle our tongues! Do you know what a bridle is? It's that strappy head and mouth piece put on a horse used to control where it should go.[45] I've seen those on horses, and they look incredibly uncomfortable! They are always biting on them and twitching their lips because it seems to

---

[45] I know, I could have Googled the exact definition, but I'm feeling a bit lazy.

be digging into their cheeks and making it difficult for their tongue to move.

I have a very fast tongue. Sometimes it's faster than my logic. Now, on occasion, God has used this to cut to the heart of a problem in someone's life, confront sin, identify issues, and defend others. If it is used outside of God, however, it can leave a whole lot of hurt feelings behind it. I recognize this in myself. As I review the Bible I've had since 7th grade, it's filled with underlined verses that I have prayed over and cried over about my tongue.

I have turned to the Bible to understand how I should use my tongue because nothing else helps me bring true peace and reconciliation. For those of us who struggle with anger, there are times when we can start to feel the onset signs approaching. It takes discipline to recognize this and do something about it. Doing something about it doesn't mean we always hide anger and never talk about conflict, however.

Ephesians 4:25-27
> *25 Therefore, laying aside falsehood, speak truth each one of you with his neighbor, for we are members of one another. 26 Be angry, and yet do not sin; do not let the sun go down on your anger, 27 and do not give the devil an opportunity.*

Here's something my incredibly patient husband has taught me about anger. Sometimes it is useful. If we look back in verse 19, it says be slow to speak and slow to anger! It doesn't say, "never get angry." That would be impossible! God has given us anger as an emotion to experience, and sometimes He uses it to help us identify when there is a problem with something. Even God had righteous anger towards the Israelites at times.

Ephesians tells us that we need to speak the truth to our neighbor, but it also says when we are angry, we should not sin. There will be times when you will exhibit the emotions of anger while having a discussion with someone else. God can use anger to signify the seriousness of a situation, but we should not hold onto anger for a long time or act out of it. The sun going down signifies a short amount of time that you get to be angry. If you keep it longer, it actually has physical effects to your body and quickly turns to bitterness or resentment. You can let people know what they did made you angry. It's not right, however, to choose sin while you are angry. It's pretty easy to recognize this sin when you intentionally do or say things to hurt another person in the moment.

I have been working on this part of my heart for years. YEARS. I still mess up. Whatever it is that you're "losing it" on, God knows. What He desires for us is a heart of humility and love. We don't just get that by agreeing with the Bible. You have to daily seek His word and practice it. We must seek to be doers of the word. We also must seek to make it right. We cannot let the sun go down on our anger.

We need to be very careful to avoid justifying our anger because we are sinners. Even if I think it helped the end result of a situation, there is always more people could have learned if I were to have responded in genuine love. No one is ever justified in sinning, no matter what has led up to it (See the entire chapter of Romans 6). The payment for sin is always death (Rom. 6:23). Praise God that He still chooses to use us, even though we are sinners! Praise God that He can change our hearts if we continually seek Him.

In business, there will be times that people cause us frustration and anger. Losing it might be something that you struggle with. I commonly find losing it doesn't always happen in front of the person I am upset with, but it happens in my car, or with family afterwards. This is still wrong. The unfortunate thing about business, however, is that you can get away with leaving unresolved conflict easier than you can with your family. We also can be guilty of addressing conflict without actually seeking to reconcile the situation in peace.

The hard part about working through the conflict for reconciliation before God and with other people: You cannot seek to reconcile without humility.

The reality is, getting angry and losing it will happen sometimes because we are human. We're not perfect, but God can still turn it around. He does this through the recognition of our failures and helping us have the humility to make it right. I cannot say this enough to myself and to you, "Humility comes with an apology." It's not always your fault that something happened. However, after an entire semester of interpersonal communication studies, I can confidently tell you, any relationship has more than one person involved. The response you have to a situation that involves another person is completely your fault.

In business, we commonly fail to push ourselves in humility. In business, it is acceptable to not apologize if you are in charge. Conflict happens regularly. The sun should not go down on your anger. Let God use your mistakes for His glory. Someday, when you stand before God, He will look at your life, and there will be no room for you to say, "Well, I only did that because this happened first." Your sin is your sin. It doesn't matter what anyone else did.

I feel the need to reiterate that your apology is necessary for the times in which you lose it. Whether it's to people in your family or to people you work with, you must be humble enough to apologize for what you did that was wrong. We commonly choose to avoid apologizing because we fear it could discredit the situation as an issue that contributed to our decision to lose it. This is an unfounded reason for refusing to humble yourself in apology regarding your reaction to the situation.

I know that I am right there with you in hating these words, but it is the truth. We must be doers of the word and not only hearers. An apology is an action that requires one to do something. An apology can also be known as a confession of sin. God calls us to do this (James 5:16; Proverbs 28:13). When we confess our sin, God can use it for His glory.

Here are a few questions that I find are very insightful to ask myself after I have lost it.

- Before I opened my mouth, did I ask myself : "Would God want me to introduce the issue I want to discuss right now?"
- Was "how" I said it the true problem in "what" I said while communicating?
- Have I only surrounded myself by people who agree with me?
- Do I have people speaking truth into this situation regardless of if I want to hear it, or have I completely secluded myself from people who could disagree with me while I process my actions?
- Where have I placed my identity?
- If I had firmly trusted that God was in control of everything to work for His glory, including in this situation, would I have responded the same way?

Today:

- Praise God for the work He is doing in your own life.
- Thank Him for paying for your sin.
- Ask Him to reveal to you the areas in your life that you are losing it.
- Pray for conviction in your heart to see the sin without justifying your actions.
- Pray that he would give you the humility to apologize when you are wrong.
- Ask God to help you quickly recognize when you are angry, and help keep you from sinning.
- Pray that God will help you deal with your anger before the sun goes down. If you have any anger today, you need to ask God how you can go about resolving it peacefully and respectfully.
- Repent of the moments you have failed to apologize after you have lost it.
- Praise God that He can display His love through us when we act humbly.

DAY 25

The Holy Spirit Does Not Use Manipulation

Spiritual manipulation runs rampant within Christian businesses and nonprofits alike. When I was in my kitchen thinking about writing on this topic, my dog started barking at the mailwoman. In my mailbox, was a letter addressed "Resident - To a Friend."

Pasted all over the front of the envelope were big words that had underlined sections. It read, "God's Holy Spirit instructed us to loan you this to start turning things around **for you.** So, here it is. Use it and be blessed." Inside was information on how I could send them some money "in faith" in order to patiently wait for the major financial blessing God had in store for me to "turn things around." Because planting my seed today would bring me blessings tomorrow!

Spiritual manipulation is a topic that makes my blood boil every time I start to think about how sick and twisted it can become. Inside this particular envelope, was a whole bunch of brochures about how God can bless me when I act in faith. There were pictures of kids, a brand-new car, and people being healed. All I needed to do was send them some money as my "seed of faith" and lay a paper printed picture of a handkerchief under my pillow that night to start seeing the blessings God has in store for me!

Across the world, people are using the name of Christianity to get what they want from you, and many times, promise you success in return, "If you just have enough faith" or "If you just give enough money." This is disgusting and a pollution of the gospel.

I have seen people empty their life savings into these promises, and to the outside observer, it's usually pretty easy to see coming. In smaller doses, however, this type of manipulation is something we all can be guilty of doing if we aren't careful. We usually aren't targeting people's finances though. People commonly use spiritual manipulation in other circumstances to gain submission or time. I have seen people leave businesses utterly defeated because of this struggle. It is also the most common crutch of the openly Christian business owner who desires control or relentless sacrifices on behalf of the organization. Because this is such a massive struggle that is so subtle, I feel the need to give some real-life examples of how this can worded.

Keep in mind, **some** of these same statements can actually be used for encouragement, but in the contexts that they were used, this was not the case. I hate when people are vague about an issue, and I think we need to seriously check our hearts about these types of statements when they are about to come out of our mouths.

Examples of Spiritual Manipulation:

"We have a spiritual connection to God, and God didn't confirm to us what He has revealed to you. So, we're kind of wondering why you would consider leaving. Your gifts work so well in supporting this business. We don't see God calling you elsewhere, but it's your choice to make."

"You really need to work on your heart right now, because I can see that you have a problem with our leadership authority by the questions you are asking and the time you're requesting of us."

"Questioning the Lord's anointed will cause you harm. Don't question where God is leading those in charge of the business."

"We care about you so much. We see the value you bring to the company and the incredible effort you've given, but we aren't in a position to make any changes to your compensation. We appreciate everything you do, and we're praying for you."

"I take time out of my day to pray for you. Can you help with this project?" Later posts on Facebook: "When did people become so ungrateful?"

"I understand you're stressed. I get that way sometimes too. I make so many sacrifices on behalf of this business, but I know it's where God is calling us. So, I know it will be worth it!"

"Maybe we didn't hit our goals this year because we didn't have enough faith."

"We don't need to be that organized, don't you trust that God will come through?"

"Well, if God owns the business, He's not going to let anyone sue us. We'll just have to trust that the inspector won't fine us for the health code violations and that God will protect us because I just don't have time to work on that right now."

"Why are you questioning me? God told me we have to do this, so let's just do it."

"I've been seeing this idea everywhere, I think it's a sign that God wants us to be making this our priority."

Subtle Messages:

If you really wanted to help us go where God is calling us, you would put in the hours to get us there.

Self-sacrifice for this business is an offering before the Lord.

You cannot talk about conflict because it brings disunity to the business.

You are the only one that feels this way, and to be open about it will make everyone doubt your relationship with God and your commitment to the business.

Some of these statements really can be an encouragement to those who are struggling with doubt, but when heard in context of the actual situations, none of them were encouraging. Conflict and the balance of power are struggles in business that happen regularly. There will be times that employees or your family won't understand where God is leading you. Here is where I need to be completely clear, though. **No one has the right to use someone else's relationship with God to guilt them, make them feel like they aren't a "good enough" Christian, or pressure them through a "faith tactic" into doing something.**

The most common way this happens is when Christians try to use wisdom that is self-serving to encourage employees, friends, family members, or church members. James talks about this wisdom. It's not always intentional, because the justification usually makes sense when it serves our own purposes.

James 3:13-18

> *13 Who among you is wise and understanding? Let him show by his good behavior his deeds in the gentleness of wisdom. 14 But if you have bitter jealousy and selfish ambition in your heart, do not be arrogant and so lie against the truth. 15 This wisdom is not that which comes down from above, but is earthly, natural, demonic. 16 For where jealousy and selfish ambition exist, there is disorder and every evil thing. 17 But the wisdom from above is first pure, then peaceable, gentle, reasonable, full of mercy and good fruits, unwavering, without hypocrisy. 18 And the seed whose fruit is righteousness is sown in peace by those who make peace.*

James tells us that jealousy and selfish ambition are the two root causes of this type of earthly wisdom. When earthly wisdom is used to justify things we want done, its fruit is disorder and every evil thing. Many people master spiritual manipulation by using gentleness in delivering the earthy wisdom. They justify what needs to happen in their own hearts and lie to themselves about what's best for the business or for that person. When an individual responds with push back, the manipulator is commonly shocked and tries to shame that person into alignment with his or her intentions. The examples we've covered show how easy it is to use Christianity as the weapon of guilt.

Make no mistake, this is an easy trap for any Christian to fall into when conflict arises. James says this is natural to our flesh to be selfish and jealous. Justifying, "My way or the highway," by telling everyone that God told you this was His plan is manipulative. If someone has a disagreement that they would like to discuss with you, we find James telling us that responding with heavenly wisdom looks pure, peaceable, gentle, reasonable, full of mercy and good fruits, unwavering, and without hypocrisy.

Someone who questions your leadership, would like to seek confirmation about the Lord's leading in your life, raises concerns about the way things are done, or has a problem with how something was handled are all moments to check your heart's intentions before responding. James says that righteousness is the fruit of peace. We must plant peace into our conversations or we will entangle ourselves in justification and self-righteousness very quickly.

Before I leave this chapter, I want to make sure you are aware that as a business owner, you can also be easily spiritually manipulated by other people inside and outside your business. I try to openly call this out, because people who are being treated this way often struggle to identify the issue quickly. Being inside a situation of spiritual abuse can distort your perspective, making it difficult to identify where this unsettling feeling is coming from. Spiritual manipulation is a heart-wrenching battle because it plays with your view of God and causes you to feel shame in confronting the things that feel wrong even though you might not be sure what part is wrong. Paul talks about these types of people.

Romans 16:17-19

17 Now I urge you, brethren, keep your eye on those who cause dissensions and hindrances contrary to the teaching which you learned, and turn away from them. 18 For such men are slaves, not of our Lord Christ but of their

own appetites; and by their smooth and flattering speech they deceive the
hearts of the unsuspecting. 19 For the report of your obedience has reached
to all; therefore I am rejoicing over you, but I want you to be wise in what is
good and innocent in what is evil.

Paul knows that we must be wary of people who can trick us. Being open to how God is working in other Christians is important, but as we previously discussed in 1 Thessalonians 5:21, we must examine everything carefully!

In your business, you should be encouraging an atmosphere of feedback. Finding new ways to improve is important to everyone's personal development and remaining competitive within your industry. While not every decision is going to be clearly from the Lord, if anyone comes forward with a conviction or direction they think God is leading, take their concerns seriously and sincerely seek the Lord about this topic. Treating their faith with respect and honoring the Lord first in your business starts with listening to God's direction. You must make the time to pray and search the scriptures or this can easily become spiritual manipulation. If you say you're going to pray about it, do it, and follow up with that person.

There will be people or one particular person within your business that will bring up issues and problems that are happening. You need to embrace these people. It will feel uncomfortable, but if these people are willing to point out the issues within your business, you cannot punish them for it. Many times, this person is the one everyone else confides in and is the only one brave enough to speak up. Do not alienate this person for speaking up, they could be the pulse of your business. Allowing them to speak up in front of you will give you the opportunity to evaluate their intentions over time. You can observe if their intentions are self-serving or truly for the sake of the business' improvement. If it is abrasive, you can discuss their approach, but you should never silence their feedback. Those who try to make your business stronger will openly discuss issues they see if it's for the sake of making the company better. Sometimes this means you will be called out for doing things wrong. Apologize and resolve the problem. Quickly resolving the problem should be one of your main priorities to ensure your employees feel cared for. Continual silence and inaction destroys morale. There will be less complaining and more dedication. Humbly lead and be sincere.

Today:

- Pray that God would convict you of the words you use when explaining your actions and intentions. Repent of the examples you can already think of in your own life where you have used manipulation.
- Pray that God would guard your heart from spiritual manipulation and teach you to discern when others use it.
- Ask God to give you heavenly wisdom and help you to sew peace.
- Thank God that He has given us the Holy Spirit to discern when our hearts start to use earthly wisdom.
- Praise the Lord for the work He is doing in your business and in the lives of others around you.
- Thank God that He can confirm His direction to many people and give us peace in our hearts when we seek Him.

DAY 26

Seeing Money for What It Is

Money is not the pitfall of every business owner, but the Bible has a lot to say about money because it is an area of sin and foolishness for many. Because businesses run using money, it is also a topic of regular discussion for business people. To talk about biblical business without talking about the concept of money would be like having a cooking class that discussed recipes but never actually cooked.

Matthew 13:22

> *22 And the one on whom seed was sown among the thorns, this is the man who hears the word, and the worry of the world and the deceitfulness of wealth choke the word, and it becomes unfruitful.*

Jesus points to the people who focus on money and the worries of the world as the ones choking the gospel right out of their lives, thus becoming unfruitful. Yikes. This is probably why it's a scary topic for most people in business to discuss it. Nobody wants to talk money and the Bible when it comes to business because God could call you to some pretty scary things in your life.

After digging into the word of God, I think I can safely summarize that God cares about how we get money, why we want money, and what we do with money. It is not wrong for your business to make money. As a matter of fact, if you are good at what you do, you might even make a lot of money! The Bible tells us we need to work hard (2 Thess. 3:6-15), and working hard for your own business in a free trade economy usually correlates to making an income while doing it. The root issue God has with money is our heart.

Hebrews 13:5-6

5 Make sure that your character is free from the love of money, being content with what you have; for He Himself has said, "I will never desert you, nor will I ever forsake you," 6 so that we confidently say, "The Lord is my helper, I will not be afraid. What will man do to me?"

Money commonly keeps people from God. This is why the writer of Hebrews stresses being content in God, knowing that He can provide for us. Having money isn't wrong, but loving money or putting your hope in money is wrong. Business growth, setting goals, having plans, and striving to grow, are all great things, but if they are the number one focus of your heart and your business, we have ourselves an idol.

Paul tells Timothy that contentment and godliness are a gain in our lives because the people that put their focus on becoming rich fall into all kinds of traps that give them incredible grief. Read what he says about this issue in 1st Timothy 6:6-12. Be wary of its truth, because it will wreck you and your business if gone unchecked.

1 Timothy 6:6-12 & 17-19

6 But godliness actually is a means of great gain when accompanied by contentment. 7 For we have brought nothing into the world, so we cannot take anything out of it either. 8 If we have food and covering, with these we shall be content. 9 But those who want to get rich fall into temptation and a snare and many foolish and harmful desires which plunge men into ruin and destruction. 10 For the love of money is a root of all sorts of evil, and some by longing for it have wandered away from the faith and pierced themselves with many griefs.

*11 But flee from these things, you man of God, and pursue righteousness,
godliness, faith, love, perseverance and gentleness. 12 Fight the good fight of
faith; take hold of the eternal life to which you were called, and you made the
good confession in the presence of many witnesses…17 Instruct those who
are rich in this present world not to be conceited or to fix their hope on the
uncertainty of riches, but on God, who richly supplies us with all things to
enjoy. 18 Instruct them to do good, to be rich in good works, to be generous
and ready to share, 19 storing up for themselves the treasure of a good
foundation for the future, so that they may take hold of that which is life
indeed.*

Notice something else Paul tells Timothy in verses 17-19. We still see the same theme of
telling people not to put their hope in money, but Paul tells him to teach people who are rich
to do good, be generous, and ready to share. Wow! We know Jesus says that it's harder for a
camel to go through the eye of a needle than for a rich man to enter the kingdom of God, but
with God all things are possible (Mark 10:17-23). Here we see that, apparently, the
miraculous happened! Some of the followers in Timothy's church are rich!

Catch this: Paul does not condemn them for being rich. Instead, they are to use what they
have to do good and to share, while warning them not to be conceited or focus on their
riches.

So where should our focus be in business? How do we use money the way God wants us to?
Jesus gives us our priorities when it comes to money:

Luke 12:15-21 & 29-32

*15 Then He said to them, "Beware, and be on your guard against every form
of greed; for not even when one has an abundance does his life consist of his
possessions." 16 And He told them a parable, saying, "The land of a rich
man was very productive. 17 And he began reasoning to himself, saying,*

*'What shall I do, since I have no place to store my crops?' **18** Then he said, 'This is what I will do: I will tear down my barns and build larger ones, and there I will store all my grain and my goods. **19** And I will say to my soul, "Soul, you have many goods laid up for many years to come; take your ease, eat, drink and be merry."' **20** But God said to him, 'You fool! This very night your soul is required of you; and now who will own what you have prepared?' **21** So is the man who stores up treasure for himself, and is not rich toward God."..... **29** And do not seek what you will eat and what you will drink, and do not keep worrying. **30** For all these things the nations of the world eagerly seek; but your Father knows that you need these things. **31** But seek His kingdom, and these things will be added to you. **32** Do not be afraid, little flock, for your Father has chosen gladly to give you the kingdom.*

If you are seeking the kingdom of God with your business, the rest will be added to you. God provides for us! Money will control your life and business if you do not choose to put it to work for God's purposes. You must be rich towards God in your life. We must let God use our finances in the ways He sees fit.

Trusting in God's provision is no excuse for making unwise financial decisions, however. Walking by faith isn't an excuse to do other things that are contradictory to the whole of scripture. A common area I see people act foolishly in business is choosing to cling to a few verses of scripture and failing to read the rest of the Bible for guidance in making big decisions.

In business, I have reviewed a few business purchase agreements. I actually love digging through people's profit and loss statements. Sometimes, looking at the difference of financial statements between Christian business owners and non-Christian business owners is embarrassing.

We should not use faith to justify foolishness. Yes, there will be times that God asks us to step out in faith, but He will not ask us to do so flippantly. We know we must count the cost to follow Jesus, but Jesus uses finances as an example of common sense when considering a decision to follow after Him.

Luke 14:25-29

> *25 Now large crowds were going along with Him; and He turned and said to them, 26 "If anyone comes to Me, and does not hate his own father and mother and wife and children and brothers and sisters, yes, and even his own life, he cannot be My disciple. 27 Whoever does not carry his own cross and come after Me cannot be My disciple. 28 For which one of you, when he wants to build a tower, does not first sit down and calculate the cost to see if he has enough to complete it? 29 Otherwise, when he has laid a foundation and is not able to finish, all who observe it begin to ridicule him, 30 saying, 'This man began to build and was not able to finish.'*

Going after a vision that God has placed on your heart doesn't mean you immediately run with it, take out a loan to finance it, and trust God to provide. I know so many people that have jumped into God's vision so fast that they didn't take the time to plan the finances or listen for how God was telling them to go about it. Is it an act of faith? It sure is, but an act of faith must be in alignment with God's timing and approach in order to be truly effective. Anything to do with your resources is a commitment. Any way to use money should be prayerfully considered.

How you get your money and what you do with it is a pretty big deal to God. When the tax collectors and Roman soldiers asked John the Baptist what they should be doing in their life, he emphasized how doing their work justly was important.

Luke 2:12-14

> *12 And some tax collectors also came to be baptized, and they said to him, "Teacher, what shall we do?" 13 And he said to them, "Collect no more than what you have been ordered to." 14 Some soldiers were questioning him, saying, "And what about us, what shall we do?" And he said to them, "Do not take money from anyone by force, or accuse anyone falsely, and be*

content with your wages. "

Running your business fairly is incredibly important in being obedient. Do you think God cares how much money you give to Him as a sacrifice if you're doing it at the cost of your employees? I don't know where this comes from, but many Christians have subtly come across implying this statement, "Working in a Christian organization is okay to be done for pennies on the dollar because it's a sacrifice made for God." I would agree that it **can be** a sacrifice made for God.

Businessman, Brian Swanson, co-founder of HOPE 4 YOUTH, stated, "If you ask a volunteer to give you the world, it motivates them. If you ask an employee to give you the world, they think you're taking advantage of them."[46]

Last time I checked, calling someone to make sacrifices for Jesus was part of the Holy Spirit's job description. You shouldn't be building this into people's paychecks for them. Pay your employees what they are competitively worth for their time and talents!

James 5:1-4

1 Come now, you rich, weep and howl for your miseries which are coming upon you. 2 Your riches have rotted and your garments have become moth-eaten. 3 Your gold and your silver have rusted; and their rust will be a witness against you and will consume your flesh like fire. It is in the last days that you have stored up your treasure! 4 Behold, the pay of the laborers who mowed your fields, and which has been withheld by you, cries out against you; and the outcry of those who did the harvesting has reached the ears of the Lord of Sabaoth.

---

[46] Swanson, B. (2014, January 14). *Christian Leadership.* Lecture presented in Bethel University, St. Paul.

God cares about what you do with your money once you receive it. Honoring God with your money will keep it from becoming a stumbling block for you and your business.

Today:

- Pray that God would have full control of your money.
- Praise Him for blessing you with what you currently have.
- Ask Him to show you how to be obedient in justly running your business.
- Confess to God any control you have been withholding from Him in your finances.
- Ask God to teach you to use your finances wisely as you follow His voice.
- Thank God that He allows us to see Him provide for people.
- Repent of the selfish thoughts you have had about money and growing your business.
- Pray that God would help you give your finances fully into His hands.

DAY 27

The Purpose and Motivation of Giving

For-profit businesses have the exciting opportunity to give because they make money! This is probably one of the most underappreciated areas of the business world. Giving can be so much fun! Giving back to your employees and allowing them to experience God's provision with you is exciting! Giving to the Lord where He has called you allows you to praise Him for His faithfulness and blessings. Let's check out Paul's letter to the Corinthian church where he discusses a commitment they made to give a financial gift to the church of Macedonia.

2 Corinthians 9:6-15

> *6 Now this I say, he who sows sparingly will also reap sparingly, and he who sows bountifully will also reap bountifully. 7 Each one must do just as he has purposed in his heart, not grudgingly or under compulsion, for God loves a cheerful giver. 8 And God is able to make all grace abound to you, so that always having all sufficiency in everything, you may have an abundance for every good deed; 9 as it is written, "He scattered abroad, he gave to the poor, His righteousness endures forever." 10 Now He who supplies seed to the*

sower and bread for food will supply and multiply your seed for sowing and increase the harvest of your righteousness; 11 you will be enriched in everything for all liberality, which through us is producing thanksgiving to God. 12 For the ministry of this service is not only fully supplying the needs of the saints, but is also overflowing through many thanksgivings to God. 13 Because of the proof given by this ministry, they will glorify God for your obedience to your confession of the gospel of Christ and for the liberality of your contribution to them and to all, 14 while they also, by prayer on your behalf, yearn for you because of the surpassing grace of God in you. 15 Thanks be to God for His indescribable gift!

Paul says that their ministry in giving was to supply the needs of the saints and allows them an opportunity to give thanks to God financially. Because they have provided thanks to God with a tangible gift, the Macedonian church will glorify God for their open confession of the gospel.

The point of giving is not to impoverish you. Paul says this in the previous chapter.

2 Corinthians 8:12-13

12 For if the readiness is present, it is acceptable according to what a person has, not according to what he does not have. 13 For this is not for the ease of others and for your affliction, but by way of equality—

We can also see the following in verse 8 of chapter 9, "having all sufficiency in everything, you may have an abundance for every good deed." If we have decided in our heart to give, what we have to give will be sufficient for every good work. It's not about the total amount you give! It's about the heart and what God has provided you with already in order to give.

When Paul says we will be enriched in everything, he doesn't just leave it there (2 Cor. 9:11). "You will be enriched in everything for all liberality." For all liberality means **for giving.** You will be enriched to give to others. Not to keep it for yourself!

In business, God gives us our talents, time, and finances so that we can give to others. How and when we do that should be in accordance with God's direction. **Our giving should lead to the glorification of God** (2 Cor. 9:13).

Receiving God's vision in knowing how and where to give is empowering. It allows you to happily say, "yes" when the right opportunities arise. This is what the church in Corinth had done months prior when Paul told them of the opportunity to give to a church body in need. The Corinthian church offered their finances before the Lord in thanksgiving for the work He has done on the cross.

Giving should be done with the right heart motives. Remember how we reviewed that God cares about how we use money? Here are some common business examples of wrong motives for giving that we need to review.

Giving is not an opportunity for self-glorification. This one was actually an eye-opening reminder for me. In business, I've always thought of giving as a great public relations opportunity to show people what you're doing in the community. Should you do public relations? Yes, but this shouldn't be considered part of your giving. Jesus tells us how we are to give.

Matthew 6:1-4

1 "Beware of practicing your righteousness before men to be noticed by them; otherwise you have no reward with your Father who is in heaven. 2 "So when you give to the poor, do not sound a trumpet before you, as the hypocrites do in the synagogues and in the streets, so that they may be honored by men. Truly I say to you, they have their reward in full. 3 But when you give to the poor, do not let your left hand know what your right hand is doing, 4 so that your giving will be in secret; and your Father who sees what is done in secret will reward you.

Giving is not a way to atone for our sin. It is to the glory of God for us to be new creations in Christ. Nothing we do can reconcile us to God, pay for our sins, or make atonement. The price has already been paid for salvation.

Ephesians 1:7

> *7 In Him we have redemption through His blood, the forgiveness of our trespasses, according to the riches of His grace*

To expect that our giving will grant us something more before God, is an insult to Christ's sacrifice on our behalf.

Giving is not an opportunity to petition God for something we want. We should not give, hoping to gain something.

Luke 6:30-31 & 35-38

> *30 Give to everyone who asks of you, and whoever takes away what is yours, do not demand it back. 31 Treat others the same way you want them to treat you...35 But love your enemies, and do good, and lend, expecting nothing in return; and your reward will be great, and you will be sons of the Most High; for He Himself is kind to ungrateful and evil men. 36 Be merciful, just as your Father is merciful. 37 "Do not judge, and you will not be judged; and do not condemn, and you will not be condemned; pardon, and you will be pardoned. 38 Give, and it will be given to you. They will pour into your lap a good measure—pressed down, shaken together, and running over. For by your standard of measure it will be measured to you in return."*

When we give, there are rewards, but Jesus does not delineate what they tangibly look like. The verse we read earlier, "Give and it will be given to you" is more than likely referring to the preceding verse on judging, condemning, and pardoning than it is referring to money. Jesus also clearly states to expect nothing in return when you loan out money (Luke 6:35-38).

When Jesus talks about getting treasure, we find He says to lay up our treasures in heaven.[47] Paul saying you will have sufficiency in all things does not mean you will become rich. You will have what is sufficient to do good works (2 Cor. 9:8)! Paul tells the Corinthian church that through their gift they will increase the harvest of their "righteousness" (2 Cor. 9:10) He does not say we will gain anything in this lifetime for our own personal enjoyment, health, or wealth. The book of Job shows how God gives and takes away for His purposes.

To use giving as a strategy for financial gain is wrong. To give with the expectation that God will give you something back means you are doing things out of your own strength to gain blessing. This would make God's provision up to you. This takes glory from God. This is blasphemy. God does not need our money to accomplish His purposes.

Job 41:11

> *"Who has given to Me that I should repay him? Whatever is under the whole heaven is Mine.*

Giving financially is not a substitute for being an active part of your local church body. The truth is, some of you are joyfully giving of only your finances. We, in America, are so prone to giving money to help instead of doing something ourselves that it's sickening. The financial payoff for personal comfort and time is easy math for business owners. "How much do I make an hour?" versus "How much I can pay someone an hour to help out?" seems justifiable. Is it though?

God didn't call us to donate to a local charity fund that we identify with.

The Pharisees were totally fine with people doing this. *You can give your money to the church and never have to help your parents out. Just tell them you already gave to God!*

---

[47] See Matthew 6:19-21 if you want to dig into this one further.

Giving was a tradition that the Pharisees held as a good substitute for the word of God. Jesus nailed them for this.

Matthew 15:5-9

> *5 But you say, 'Whoever says to his father or mother, "Whatever I have that would help you has been given to God," 6 he is not to honor his father or his mother.' And by this you invalidated the word of God for the sake of your tradition. 7 You hypocrites, rightly did Isaiah prophesy of you: 8 'This people honors Me with their lips, But their heart is far away from Me. 9 'But in vain do they worship Me, Teaching as doctrines the precepts of men.'"*

We are called to be a part of the body of Christ. They are our spiritual family. We should be actively involved in each other's lives if we are ever going to be able to move as one body. Giving money is not an excuse to shirk the responsibilities that the word of God calls us to do.

Giving is not a substitute for a personal relationship with God. God loves a cheerful giver (2 Cor. 9:7). This would imply that your heart is connecting with joy and worship to God in the process of giving. If you give just because you think it will fulfill your need to connect with God, you're doing it wrong. There are businesses that give money to different organizations that will in turn pray for them. Some have even gone as far as actually vetting and hiring a prayer warrior to bring their business before the Lord on their behalf! We love efficiency and cost savings; therefore, we apply it to our spiritual walk with Jesus!

If we substitute ourselves before the Lord with money or paying someone else to do it for us, we are not seeking the Lord. Did you know during the time of Jesus, the Jewish people made a daily sacrifice on behalf of Caesar?[48] Covering your bases isn't seeking the Lord! This is

---

[48] Duling, D. (1982). The Jewish World of Jesus: An Overview. Retrieved from https://pages.uncc.edu/james-tabor/the-jewish-world-of-jesus-an-overview/

completely wrong! James tells us that seeking the Lord requires a whole lot of "you" action, not somebody else!

James 4:8

8 Draw near to God and He will draw near to you. Cleanse your hands, you sinners; and purify your hearts, you double-minded.

Today:

- Pray that God would help you to give joyfully.
- Repent and confess to God of the ways you have been giving with the wrong motives.
- Ask Him to show you where you should be giving to extend His glory.
- Praise God that He gives to us in order to allow us to give to others.
- Thank God that He has given us so many instructions on giving in His word.
- Praise God that He can use our giving for good works.
- Pray that God would show you how to give with thanksgiving because of Christ's work on the cross.

DAY 28

Retirement

When I was a child growing up in Minnesota, the church first taught me about the concept of snowbirds. Snowbirds are these select individuals within your congregation that normally have salt and pepper to white hair. They can be singles, couples, friends, etc. Usually right after Halloween is when we started to notice the empty pews in our church. They are with us in the summer months, but as soon as the first signs of winter approach, they travel down with the birds to warmer climates.

They spend the winter away in small communities with those who look exactly like them. Sometimes their community believes exactly the same thing they do, and they spend their time doing crafting activities to "glorify the Lord." Doing exactly what their non-Christian friends have been doing, but putting a Godly spin on it. It appears that feeling spiritually productive is the norm for these subgroups in Arizona, Texas, Florida, and the like. Some communities even host many events to gain more knowledge of the Bible. My father-in-law calls this part spiritual constipation. Much is going in, but nothing is coming out of it.

In my adult life, I find this activity to be the mass exodus of wisdom from the local church.

How many times have we seen wise individuals opt out of church eldership or do a poor job at it because half their year is not attending the church they are supposed to be leading?!

This actually is a new phenomenon. It was never the case before the Baby Boomer generation. Boomers were the first generation of youth to have marketing campaigns target them and their money. The word "teenager" was coined on their behalf. With their families deserting the farms for the city and child labor laws hitting the labor force hard, it was difficult for them to take on adult responsibilities quickly. Their free time and selfless parents became the birth of their "self-expression."

Haydn Shaw, a leading generational researcher, wrote:

> Parents and their adolescents have always irritated each other, but the adults think, It's just a phase; they'll grow out of it. But the Boomers didn't grow out of it, because society was effecting a profound shift in their focus---from sacrifice to self-fulfillment. It takes cash to become the "Me" generation, and Boomers were the first generation to have the money, time and freedom to explore self and search for meaning.[49]

Romans 6:10-14

> **10** For the death he died he died to sin, once for all, but the life he lives he lives to God. **11** So you also must consider yourselves dead to sin and alive to God in Christ Jesus. **12** Let not sin therefore reign in your mortal body, to make you obey its passions. **13** Do not present your members to sin as instruments for unrighteousness, but present yourselves to God as those who have been brought from death to life, and your members to God as instruments for righteousness. **14** For sin will have no dominion over you,

---

[49] Shaw, H. (2013). Sticking points: How to get 4 generations working together in the 12 places they come apart. Carol Stream, IL: Tyndale House.

since you are not under law but under grace.

This is not an affront to the Boomer generation. We all have started to think this way. Retirement has become the cultural equivalent of "time to do things for me." We were created to work, and through the saving grace of God, we are not to obey our sinful passions. "Doing things for me" sure sounds a lot like obeying your sinful passions! Make no mistake, **resting is Biblical.** The American concept of retirement, however, is not. Being instruments for righteousness means that we are still tools God uses.

Romans 5:6-11

> *6 For while we were still weak, at the right time Christ died for the ungodly. 7 For one will scarcely die for a righteous person—though perhaps for a good person one would dare even to die— 8 but God shows his love for us in that while we were still sinners, Christ died for us. 9 Since, therefore, we have now been justified by his blood, much more shall we be saved by him from the wrath of God. 10 For if while we were enemies we were reconciled to God by the death of his Son, much more, now that we are reconciled, shall we be saved by his life. 11 More than that, we also rejoice in God through our Lord Jesus Christ, through whom we have now received reconciliation.*

"I deserve this" is a myth. In light of the gospel, the only thing we deserve is death for our sins, but God, who is rich in mercy, chose to make the ultimate sacrifice while we were still enemies of God.

"Well done good and faithful servant" is not the acknowledgement given to us at age 65. Dave Ramsey is passionate about helping people retire with dignity. In his book, *The Total Money Makeover,* he discusses how the majority of Americans have not financially set themselves up to retire with dignity. [50]

---

[50] Ramsey, D. (2013). The Total Money Makeover (p. 142). [Place of publication not identified]: Thomas Nelson.

I wholeheartedly believe that we do need to focus on the future, and be able to retire with dignity. However, God is dignity in its ultimate form. He is all glorious and all majestic, but He can choose to use these attributes as He pleases. Nebeel Qureshi describes this concept of God to a Muslim woman in his book, *No God But One: Allah or Jesus?*. He painted a picture of the woman dressed in her finest and going to a party when she sees her own child drowning in mud. He describes how a mother would stop to save her child, even if it meant getting dirty and showing up to the party late. In the same way, God has dignity and willingly chose to lay it aside to save us from our sin.[51]

Philippians 2:5-8

> **5** *Have this mind among yourselves, which is yours in Christ Jesus,* **6** *who, though he was in the form of God, did not count equality with God a thing to be grasped,* **7** *but emptied himself, by taking the form of a servant, being born in the likeness of men.* **8** *And being found in human form, he humbled himself by becoming obedient to the point of death, even death on a cross.*

Having dignity in retirement is not wrong, but choosing to live for yourself is. Retiring might mean joining multiple boards and mentoring young business people. It might mean going into the world to preach the gospel or supporting those who do with your prayers, wisdom, and finances. It might mean guiding your children or being a caregiver for your grandchildren. Whatever God calls you to do in retirement, I can guarantee that it won't be for you.

Paul writes a letter to Titus telling him what the qualifications of an elder are to be in the church. Part of it was to be, "holding fast the faithful word which is in accordance with the teaching," so that he will be able both to exhort in sound doctrine and to refute those who

---

[51] Qureshi, N. (2016). *No God but one: Allah or Jesus?* Grand Rapids: Zondervan.

contradict (Titus 1:9).

At this specific time, Titus was dealing with some Jewish people who were polluting the gospel, "They profess to know God, but by *their* deeds they deny *Him*," (Titus 1:16). In the very next part of the letter, Paul clearly lays out what older people are supposed to be doing.

Titus 2:2-5

> *2 Older men are to be temperate, dignified, sensible, sound in faith, in love, in perseverance. 3 Older women likewise are to be reverent in their behavior, not malicious gossips nor enslaved to much wine, teaching what is good, 4 so that they may encourage the young women to love their husbands, to love their children, 5 to be sensible, pure, workers at home, kind, being subject to their own husbands, so that the word of God will not be dishonored.*

The gospel is not completed until the day of Christ. Investing in others and knowing the word of God to refute false doctrine is part of your purpose. You have more wisdom than you realize, you have seen God work more than you can remember, and you are not off the hook from continuing the kingdom of God upon retirement.

Did you know that the 1040 window does not allow the visa status of "missionary?" These countries where evangelism is illegal are the hard, dangerous places of the world that are not on most people's vacation lists. It's no wonder that the majority of our missions funding goes to places that already have access to the gospel. We enjoy giving and visiting them when we have time off!

Countries with no access to the gospel, no written word translated in their language, no Christians that they could ever meet in person, are also desperate for an economic boost. Most of these countries allow for the visa status of "retired." They also allow visa statuses for "business consultant," "investor," "board member," and "owner/operator."

Do you realize that what you know as a business owner is one of the most desired economic skill sets of the unreached world? We have people graduating from seminary with loads of biblical knowledge, but they are not welcome in this world. Businesses bring value. Businesses bring jobs. Businesses bring relationships. You might not consider yourself an evangelist, but we are all commanded to be.

For those of you that feel like you will go insane if you ever retire because you need to work, PRAISE GOD! He is not done with you anyway.

While your soul still remains in your body, you are called to be an image bearer of Christ. This last year, my husband was asked to play the cello for a fellow cello player, Denise Hohl, who was on hospice. Cancer had invaded her body and she and her husband knew the end was near. We came to their house, played music, and I watched them praise the Lord together. In the face of death, with the knowledge that she would soon be with her Savior, they joyfully praised the Lord together through tears.

I praise the Lord for them. I was only with them for an hour, and I saw a glimpse of the divine peace and joy our God can give us. I saw a couple that praised the Lord in death and magnified His name regardless of the time left. It was precious, it was beautiful, and it changed my perspective of marriage entirely. Regardless of where we are in pain, in sickness, in life, in mobility, in cognitive capacity, or in finances, God can still glorify His name in your life. Prayer and intercession are two of the most powerful weapons you can wield for the gospel. They can be done from anywhere, and by anyone.

As you plan your future, run your business to glorify the Lord, and pursue Him with your whole heart, pray your life would end with people looking at how wonderful the Lord is, magnifying His name. Pray that you would be able use your retirement for the purpose of the gospel. Pray that He would reveal to you how you can prepare your business now for this to happen effectively. Thank Him for His love toward us in laying aside His dignity to save us. Thank Him for delivering you from the penalty of your sin. Praise Him for His continual grace in your life.

Today:

- Find that paper where you wrote down what you think God has called you to in Day 3.
- How has God changed your initial perspectives or refined you in this plan?
- Praise God that He is still working in you as you move through every new stage of life and business.

I will leave you with the words of Paul, praying that God will sustain you to the end because of His faithfulness.

1 Corinthians 1:4-9

> *4 I give thanks to my God always for you because of the grace of God that was given you in Christ Jesus, 5 that in every way you were enriched in him in all speech and all knowledge— 6 even as the testimony about Christ was confirmed among you— 7 so that you are not lacking in any gift, as you wait for the revealing of our Lord Jesus Christ, 8 who will sustain you to the end, guiltless in the day of our Lord Jesus Christ. 9 God is faithful, by whom you were called into the fellowship of his Son, Jesus Christ our Lord.*

Thanks for reading! Please add a short review on Amazon, and let me know what you thought!

About the Author

R. N. Anderson is a business strategist, tactical economist, writer, speaker, human capital investor, educator, mom to many, and wife to one. She helps business owners review their current investments to ensure cost-effectiveness. She is passionate about accountability and processes that can help business owners grow and market their business efficiently. She is also passionate about Jesus, dogs, children, good food, and learning anything people are willing to teach her.

She and her husband reside in Minnesota with a fluctuating herd of children and their dog. Her other published titles are currently not available for mass distribution. They include: *103 Things to Fit in Your Belly Button[52]* and *My First Cookbook*.

To request additional information about this book, speaking opportunities, or other inquiries please email: 28daystoabiblicalbusiness@gmail.com

---

[52] Fact, in my adult life, I met the owner of the printing business who published this work for me, and I was too embarrassed to mention it. I'm sure it holds a forever place in that graphic designer's memory. However, I did check "becoming a published author" off my list early in life! Wondering if those are both sarcastic books? Yes, this is a joke. You can chuckle.

Acknowledgments

There are a few people who have helped to make this book a reality, and I cannot thank them enough for their impact on my life, hard work, guidance, and prayers. My husband, thank you for being so supportive and going before the Lord with me continually. I am so grateful for the joy you have blessed me with. Jael, thank you for being a spiritual mentor in my life. My mom, you have continually inspired me to love and get excited about the word of God. My grandfather, for teaching me what it means to be relentless in serving others joyfully. My sister, your prayers have been so valuable.

Brian H., you pushed me to think hard through Biblical issues in the work place and in my personal life. David H., who took the time to guide my young mind so long ago. MaryAnn H., for helping me fall in love with business. Leo G., for putting up with my sassiness and forcing me to reconcile finances with accountability. Brad A. for being the first to show me how to apply the Bible to business in a tactical way. It changed my life.

Praise the Lord that He is not finished with me yet!

www.ingramcontent.com/pod-product-compliance
Lightning Source LLC
Chambersburg PA
CBHW060320050426
42449CB00011B/2575